I AM ALSO A VOICE

A Freedom from Social Oppression Anthology:
Creation of a Unique Racial Identity

Michael Holloway King, M.D.

Author of

Hide and Play Dead:
From Memoir to Real-Time Healing

And

Overcoming Oppression:
Your Guide to a New Life

I AM ALSO A VOICE A Freedom from Social Oppression Anthology: CREATION OF A UNIQUE RACIAL IDENTITY is a work of non-fiction. Ideas have been given proper attribution and credit throughout the work. Any resemblance to other works is unintentional.

PREFACE

I am pleased to present the *first* of four anthologies, or collection of narrative pieces from my first book, "Hide and Play Dead." The organizing theme for this anthology is *racial identity*. As a mixed-race person, racism permeated my entire life, in a skewed and extreme manner, due to the transgenerational passage of slave-based childrearing practices among the black intelligentsia and aristocracy.

My experience is complex, but this collection strives to make all as transparent as possible, and leave the remainder for reading a complete work or to future writing. My second book, "Overcoming Oppression," allows a profound immersion experience into the nature of racism and its effect on persons of a different complexion than the predominant white social strata.

Although the reading here flows with the narrative, it cannot truly compare to reading the original text with all its segments and its format as a cohesive nonfiction novel—with building suspense, balancing light or metaphysical elements, and climactic pinnacles. Footnotes have been removed, and explanatory bridging sentences inserted instead, to preserve continuity to the subject of racism.

You will also note that, due to my effort to heal my own post-traumatic stress disorder while writing the book, I include insightful "flashbacks" and bridging metaphors that may seem incongruent within this text, but would be easily understood in the book. Please use your insight wherever "gaps" may appear, as they are full of innuendo and meaning in any format, whether in the original work or as discrete short stories.

The content here may be of great value for high school, college or university courses in several fields—including sociology, psychology, anthropology, history, English, cross-cultural—and of course, African American studies. I urge younger readers to suggest some of the following material to their professors or teachers, and for academicians to take a second look at what is revealed in these pages.

I hope that readers will not only read the entirety of "Hide and Play Dead," but also "Overcoming Oppression." Racism and

prejudice are harbingers of the neoslavery that looms on our horizon. Feel free to visit my website and blog at www.michaelhollowayking.com, to leave comments or communicate with me directly through the blog pages, especially about the topics that this or my other works may pose.

I welcome writings from others to include in my blog and social media forums, for we are all facing the advent of neoslavery and oppression in an emerging two-class social structure. But we are not alone, and I believe that the battle for freedom will succeed by non-violent social resistance to the corporate and social elite… Especially if awareness of an exit from the very essence of shame and oppression that I have uncovered is disseminated among the public.

The other anthologies in this series center on the topics of *individuation, sexuality,* and a metaphysical and inspirational anthology, focused on *spirituality.*

TABLE OF CONTENTS

The second chapter of "Hide and Play Dead" is a composite of my ancestral roots. The chapter's opening, *The Night Gallery,* stands out as an example of poetic prose.

THE NIGHT GALLERY

I don't know when I began to hear the ancestral drumbeats. Some people with tinnitus hear ringing in their ears. Those with an aneurysm in their neck or brains hear the gushing blood of their pulse. But the rhythm and pace of my drumbeats are a precise reflection of my emotions. They stem from the heart, itself.

I'm at my desk—piles of disorganized notes surround me in my little study. Ideas flash like lightning in my mind. I write and type with an unbridled passion. I will spend most of the next six sleepless months held captive in the cage of my past, thrashing against the confines of my psyche.

But for now, it's time to get some rest.

I have had insomnia since I was seven or eight years old. I am afraid to fall asleep. Though, to the observer at home, I was sleeping "like an angel," or outside, "acting like a saint," inside I felt like I was "hiding and playing dead" for instinctual survival by averting the eyes of predators. I was in a chronic state of terrified hyper-vigilance, waiting for the next boundary violation—starting with my door being thrown open or a knife poised at my neck.

I try to dissociate into a dream state as I finally lay myself down to sleep. My dreams are often terrifying like the Loch Ness monster emerging from the murky depths. I worry about what tortured specters will emerge from my subconscious when I let down the protective guard of my mental filter.

My brother is one of them.

"Now I lay me down to sleep. If I die before I wake, I pray the Lord my soul to take." This was my prayer ritual as a child. On Saturday nights, I would say it twice for extra protection. Saturday nights my parents allowed my brother and me to stay up late and watch TV: "The Alfred Hitchcock Show," "The Twilight Zone," "The Night Gallery," and "Creature Features." My brother would wait until I was frozen and breathless with terror to shout, "BOO!" in my face and shove me to the floor.

I remember struggling to stay awake and prove my courage, waiting until my brother fell asleep first, and then watching TV until 2am when the broadcasting finally ended. I couldn't let my brother call me a coward, a scaredy-cat, a sissy.

My nightmares started after seeing the movie, "The Pit and the Pendulum," with its depiction of human abuse and torture. If I close my eyes, I can still see the Iron Lady, the shackles and bars, and the ultimate sacrificial platform upon which the victim was bound and watching a huge blade swing back-and-forth, slowly ratcheting down to slice open his belly.

My family moved from a tiny third-floor apartment in the city to a remote house in the countryside when I was six years old. The house was equipped with a huge foghorn, which was necessary to signal my brother and me to come home from the vast woodlands behind our house.

My brother loved to terrorize me in the forest, too. He would prod me to climb up a tall tree, nudging me from beneath, and promising to catch me should I fall. When I'd reached unwieldy branches, and felt sufficiently nervous, he would scamper down as fast as he could and run away— leaving me pleading for help. Other times, he would escort me deep into the forest and veer from the usual path, until I was lost. Then he'd suddenly vanish as I dashed back and forth, frantically calling his name. My petrified images would then chill me to the bone… "Hansel and Gretel are left lost in the woods for the witch's oven."

At night, alone in my bedroom, I always had to check the closet several times. "Monsters, Inc." … Something always seemed to be lurking in my closet. I experimented with the door closed, then wide open, and eventually decided that half-open was the least disturbing. Then I lay in bed with my eyes half-open for hours, listening to my parents talking through the walls. In the muffled murmur of their voices, I could hear with uncanny acuity if either my name or my brother's—Roy, Junior—was mentioned. I could monitor the crescendo and decrescendo of their voices, like my mother's piano playing. I was always prepared for the moment when the music-playing of their voices became forte and the cords banged and broke into cacophony—when my door would be thrown wide open, the light turned on, and I would be interrogated and chastised for any imperfect behavior.

"Why did you *wait* until after dark to walk the dog, Michael?"

I do not remember sleeping as a child. I only remember *pretending* to be asleep, imagining I was an innocent sleeping angel.

Today, my monsters come in several forms.

The scariest are the phantoms and ghosts; they cannot be frightened by the threat of death, for they are already dead. They cannot be exposed and, therefore, they have neither shame nor guilt. They cannot be controlled without fear or shame—and that's what makes them so scary. When I try to fall asleep, they emerge from some tortured and deeply repressed part of myself.

And then, there is the Invisible Man who appears during the daytime, leaving only footprints in the snow. He can be benign, but he's unpredictable. Sometimes, he just plays tricks on me—like the cartoon character, "Casper the Ghost," who mystifies mortals for fun. Other times, he is stealthy and treacherous—like Gollum in "The Lord of the Rings," who manipulates another's pity to steal and selfishly risk their lives. He can turn on me without warning; he could stab me in the back, or strangle me from the front. All I can see then is the weapon— a rope, a knife, or perhaps a racist custom or local law, but not the person that threatens my existence.

The Invisible Man's eyes used to stare at me when I walked to school as a child. He is still incarnate and untouchable. His abuse is solipsistic, engulfing me like masters using their house slaves. His presence is cold, insidious, subtle, and undetectable.

He is white.

There is the Boogie Man who appears in the shadowy twilight. He is hideous and carnal. His semi-solid form is dark, solid yet mushy. His surface is wet, like thick sweat or mucus. His appearance is as black as the night itself. He is menacing and creepy, and follows me as closely as my own shadow. He is as putrid as my own tar-filled lungs. He is as violent as the field slave who stabs his master in the back while he is sleeping. There's an old derogatory term for those whose dark skin makes them undetectable at night.

He is a spook.

Then, there are the Restless Bones of the Dead. They are the skeletons of the walking dead of my own ancestors whose haunting past pervades my thoughts both day and night. They are comprised of images and "memories" passed on to me through generations of storytelling.

My mother loved to read children's stories to Roy, Junior and me. The classics, like Grimm's Fairy Tales, were disturbing. They depicted sadistic child abuse and tormented creatures, and they rarely had a happy ending. At first, I sat on my mother's lap; then, as I grew older, I sat on her knee; and then I sat on the floor at her feet. At some point, when I was about six or seven years old, she began to be unable to finish the stories. I would see her look far away and start to cry. Then she would apologize and go to her bedroom where she cried louder, but behind her locked door. Other times, she would tell me her own story, or stories of my ancestors.

Even in my childhood, I understood why her worst nightmares started in childhood after seeing the debut of the movie, "King Kong."

MY MOTHER'S PATERNAL LINEAGE
THE FIELD SLAVES

My mother's paternal lineage, the Holloways, has been traced far back to about the year 1700. The Holloway story starts with "Phillip", my *grandfather's, grandfather's grandfather*. Phillip's fine, aquiline features that were passed down indicate he had Arabic-African roots, probably from West Central Africa. His homeland, Mali, was renowned for a golden age of literacy, with universities and scholarly centers like Timbuktu. Per later historical evidence, he most likely spent his youth in a cosmopolitan and settled culture of tribal customs and family ties, of communal life and traditional ritual. Even slaves in Mali played an important role as royal administrators and soldiers.

But Phillip, like many other Malian leaders, scholars and soldiers, was ambushed, snatched and ripped from his roots by the increasing human plunder of the period. It has been estimated that sixty-nine percent of all African people transported in the Transatlantic Slave Trade from 1517–1700 AD were from West Central Africa. The thousand-mile march to the coast, shackled around the neck, under whip and gun, was a death march in which two of every five blacks died, and many more would die before arriving at the auction block in Georgia.

Phillip was a rebellious runaway field slave in the early 1700s. He was kept in captivity on the Holloway plantation for a few years, during which time he produced several children. Then he devised a clever scheme to vanish into the night. He is depicted in his grandson's autobiography as strong-willed and capable of living in total hermitage, hidden in the forests of Georgia. My ancestor evaded capture for over a decade, but was finally apprehended and received the usual punishment—torture, and probably death by overwork.

I imagine Phillip idly fishing under a thatched-roof lean-to on the banks of a shallow river. Slave bounty hunters have followed the smoke from his pit fireplace. Suddenly, a half-dozen armed men and barking hounds crush through the branches of trees and bushes across the stream.

Phillip starts to run—but it's too late this time. A bullet is fired. "STOP, NIGRA, OR DIE!" Within minutes, Phillip is shackled and his branded body is identified as property of the huge Holloway Plantation.

"What's your name, slave?" demands one of his captors.

"Phillip is my English name," he says with pride.

"Your name is *NIGRA* Phillip! Your master is *MISTER* Holloway. We've been hunting you for a very long time. But you ain't got luck or smarts on your side this time, Nigra. Mister Holloway wants you back, dead or alive."

The bounty hunter spits on my great-great-great great grandfather's defiant face. He cannot wipe it away for his hands are tied together. His ankles are then shackled with iron manacles and chains. He is bound to a tree where he is burned with torches, mutilated with knives, beaten with clubs, and furiously whipped.

He glares at the captor as he is unshackled and shoved into a metal cage on a barge. He is banging and clawing at the mesh, howling in pain like a wild animal. He rips off his tattered rags to stop the bleeding from his missing ear and digits—and perhaps a mutilated nose, lips, or genitals.

"He'll get 150 lashes back at the plantation, I guess," says one of his captors.

"Think he'll survive?" opines another.

"Maybe, but he's lost a lot of blood."

"Bet he'll die already from infection."

When Phillip arrives back at the plantation, several hundred slaves are gathered and forced to watch his mortal punishment. Except for the sound of the lashings, there is total silence as he is martyred. By tradition, a red bandana covers the stump of his missing ear. Blood soaks the tattered shreds of his pants and no skin remains on his back.

He lapses into unconsciousness at the 80th stroke of the whip and collapses in shock from pain and blood loss. The last image many may have had of my ancestor was like that of Christ: Phillip is dangling from his wrists that are bound high up on the whipping post, his limp knees hover just above the blood-drenched dirt, and he is not breathing.

If he survives, without modern-day transfusions and antibiotics, the torture will continue. Perhaps he will be stripped naked, bent over and chained by both his hands and feet to a short stake in the ground without shelter, or forced to walk and drown on the water wheel, or hung in a tree and left to die from dehydration. He is too old to endure the agony of hard labor that welcomes him home. He is too old to be useful.

But he has left offspring who will remember his name and his courageous struggle for freedom.

*

Phillip's grandson, Houston Hartsfield Holloway, was also a slave on the Holloway Plantation. Like all slaves, he was forbidden to learn to read or write by one of the strictest laws, which prohibited slave literacy. The laws were designed to conceal historical atrocities and prevent slave uprisings; an educated black might realize how horribly he was treated and revolt. It also precluded documentation of kinship ties to white masters and their families.

The harshest abuse of the entire history of slavery demanded the erasure and silencing of African Americans. Slave voices were discredited or omitted. Literacy threatened the fictional depiction of the Negro. Slaves were defined as mentally inferior non-humans that did not exist as individuals with subjective experiences or feelings; they were only imbued with a dangerous sexuality.

Like runaway slaves, *literate* slaves suffered similar, severe punishment for this "crime." They were threatened with being sold "down the river" and away from their families, and they were treated as harshly as runaway slaves, with savage beatings to the amputation of ears, fingers and toes, or worse.

Only a few slaves wrote narratives, which, when published, powerfully exposed the evils of slavery. Houston continued the rebellious heritage of his grandfather. In clandestine secrecy and in mortal fear of the risk he took, he succeeded to become literate and wrote his story.

I imagine Houston struggling to decipher and memorize the written words from a stolen book, perhaps by candlelight, late after midnight when all were safely asleep. How long it took to write and where he hid the work is unknown. In the end, his precious autobiography was soon forgotten as "junk"; the manuscript was shoved into a paper bag and lost in one of my great aunt's huge attics. It was stumbled upon after her death, more than a century after Houston wrote it.

The Library of Congress hurriedly acquired the work. They said they were shocked by its discovery and the insight it provided. They knew of no comparable document in existence. The work has recently been published under the title, "In His Own Words," edited by David E. Patterson, a Brown University professor of history.

Houston Hartsfield Holloway
My maternal great-great-grandfather

Since slaves were only half human, and two-thirds vote's worth—a vote granted to their owner—they could have neither an official state marriage, nor a church-sanctioned marriage. Houston wrote that he begged his master, Mr. Holloway, for permission to marry. He was filled with joy when he was finally allowed to "jump the broom" and have children.

But Houston was forced into separation from his wife and children, who lived on another plantation. He was only allowed to visit his family on Sundays when they would meet to go to church, and then—like every other day—he'd collapse in achy exhaustion after limitless hours of hard labor and a greasy evening meal. Houston also wrote about the joy of being freed, for in later life after Emancipation, he finally became a free man.

Houston, the freed slave, begot John Wesley Holloway, a charismatic scholar, preacher, and published poet. Among the books written by John Wesley Holloway are "From the Desert" (1919) and "The Book of American Negro Poetry" (1922). He begins the former work depicting his slave ancestors dying off in the late 1800s.

I AM A VOICE

I am the voice of a race of men
Who lie at the point of death;
I hold mine ear to their fainting lips,
To catch their dying breath.
I gather up the songs they sang
And the words they had to say,
To hoard them till the coming time
Brings in a better day.

I write it down—the tale of woe
My mother used to tell;
Record my father's story, too,
Who stood his bondage well.
I sing the song of the cabin home
And the banjo on the wall;
I catch the prayer of the sighing saint
To whom "de Lawd" was all.

They one by one have laid them down
In a low plantation grave,
Till rarely one of the host is found
Who says, "I was a slave."

Excerpted from the introduction of
"From the Desert."
The Neale Publishing Company: 1919.

John Wesley begot my *grandfather*, Herbert Milo Holloway, professor of mathematics at the "colored-only" Fisk University. He carried on the family tradition of rebelliousness well. Herbert Milo begot Estelle Marie Holloway, my mother. And I inherited "Holloway" as my middle name.

*

My grandfather was a very strict, sullen, and perhaps depressed man. His nearly jet-black complexion, intense eyes, and tall, proud stature all converged to make him look distinguished. As a child, I would look up to "Granddaddy" and feel awed by the stern, brute force he seemed to embody and contain. Later, I understood why Mom's nightmares began after seeing "King Kong." Grandpa Holloway never smiled, and chose his few words carefully. He was a consummate intellectual with a vast library of literature, along with his collection of all that was known at that time about mathematics. He was also an accomplished violinist and photographer.

Herbert Milo Holloway
My Maternal Grandfather

His only sibling, called "Uncle Guerney" by the whole family, was a doctor. He was among the first Negroes to have ever taken studies at my own medical school, Harvard. But it was the 1920s and Guerney was separated from the white students by a thick wire grate "for mutual protection." It was like being in a cage, he once told me.

My grandfather came to visit his daughter's family in the North every summer. He would tow his small motorboat up from Nashville to take my brother and me fishing on Lake Erie, leaving my grandmother with my parents at home.

I am seven years old, sitting on the front passenger seat of Grandpa's Buick. Grandpa fixes his eyes on the road in tomb-like silence. I feel small and frightened and I ask him no questions. I can barely endure sitting in mute stillness for several hours, from the car to the boat to the car again.

I don't know how to fish and when Grandpa sees a tugging on my line, he commands me, "Reel it in!" The perch is flopping desperately on the boat's floor and the hook is lodged in its eye. I feel so sorry for the helpless, maimed creature that I cannot touch it. Annoyed, Grandpa yanks the hook out, pulling the eye with it, and puts the twitching corpse along with the others on his chain.

My eyes gaze into the murky water and I wonder how deep it is and what scary monsters inhabit the underwater world below me....

Grandpa was a *proud* man, perhaps arrogant, and he was not afraid to challenge whites or even show his rage to them. As a professor at the white-funded Fisk University, he was considered *too* proud for the school's reputation of producing meek, intellectual colored people. Consequently, he was denied raises and promotions as punishment, and lived in near poverty.

Granddaddy could hold his head high, even when spat upon in public. The family lived in squalor in an attic without running water for several years, before Grandpa Holloway built his brick house with his own hands.

Grandpa was also an *angry* man; trapped deep inside was a core of frustration and hatred. He died of a heart attack at age sixty-five, only a few months after he retired from teaching. I remember my mother telling me that whites that knew of him feared his wrath and loathed his pride. One day, bullets pierced the walls of the attic where Grandpa, Grandma, and my mother lived; it was clearly a warning to not keep crossing the line.

My mother also told me that the scariest moment of her life happened late one evening as Grandpa was driving his car on a suburban street in Nashville. His wife sits next to him daydreaming, and my eight-year-old mother is sitting quietly on the back seat.

Suddenly a flashy car passes them at a reckless speed, honking its horn. The white driver yells at Grandpa, "Stupid dumb Nigger! Get off the road!"

"Now, I'm going to *kill* that Honky," Grandpa mutters.

He snaps from latent rage to murderous impulse. His usual scowl instantly transforms into a pursed lip, red-eyed squint, with his fists locked in a stone-like clench around the steering wheel. His foot jams the accelerator full-throttle and a mad chase after the white driver begins.

Grandma snaps out of her reveries into panic. She looks at her husband's face, which is so familiar and yet suddenly unrecognizable. She implores and begs, "Herbie, no—*don't!* For God's sake, Herbie, *stop!*" She places her hands on the wheel and tries to turn it, but she is no match against Grandpa's brute force.

"Yep. I'M GOING TO KILL HIM!" Grandpa repeats.

My mother is petrified, breathing the air of violence and death. She joins her mother, imploring, "Daddy, please stop! I'm so scared. Stop!" Her little hands tug desperately on Grandpa's collar.

"Think about your child, Herbie!" Grandma begs.

Suddenly, the white man's car brakes directly in front of him. Grandma can now turn the wheel so that their car runs onto the curb. Grandpa jams his brakes into a screeching halt to avoid crashing into a lamppost. The white man drives on. My grandfather pounds the dashboard and then collapses in silence over the steering wheel.

The incident will never be mentioned again.

MY MOTHER'S MATERNAL LINEAGE
THE HOUSE SLAVES

For over a hundred years after Emancipation, the house slave and mixed-race minority carried both status and financial advantages. But such privileges came with a very steep price tag.

Survival for house slaves demanded flawless obedience to convention and authority. They were forced to "read their master's mind" and meet his unspoken wants and expectations. House slaves were mere extensions of the master and his family, who saw them as objects to be exploited for personal gratification. And incestuous, or near incestuous, boundary violations became normal.

Once, when I was four years old, my mother told me this story, passed down through many generations. It's the story of a house slave ancestor who served as the master's nanny. "The nanny was very old and had a weak heart," my mother said. "She began to fall asleep instead of watching over her master's children. So, her master put splintered toothpicks in her eyes to prop them open."

Thanks to cross-generational stories and corroborated by numerous historical facts, it appears that my maternal grandmother's Johnson lineage is traced back to a single moment in the mid-1800s. My maternal grandmother's grandmother was nicknamed "Evelina." Evelina was a twelve-year-old slave girl who was impregnated by her master. She belonged to a man destined to become the 17th president of the United States— Andrew Johnson.

"Massah Johnson is drunk, Evelina—*be careful.*" Evelina's mother advises, while cooking in the big house kitchen. Evelina is a shy and obedient girl, with reddish hair and an olive complexion. She has never known her biological father.

Vice-president Andrew Johnson took office upon the assassination of Abraham Lincoln. He was from Tennessee and he was a slave-owner. He was also a notorious drunkard who could barely stand up for his inauguration, and certainly one of the most incompetent presidents in American history. He looted the South after the Civil War, ruining Lincoln's plans for a judicious Reconstruction, and presumably profited greatly from his misdeeds before his impeachment.

Andrew Johnson appears at the kitchen door. He leans against the doorframe, leering at the girl. He comes up to her and fondles her pubertal breasts.

"*Please*, Massah! Leave her alone!" the mother begs. Then she whispers, "She's your *daughter!*"

The soon-to-be American President mutters, "It's my *property!* My grandfather had your grandmother, and that's the way it is. We're doing your children a favor. We're making them more human!"

He pulls Evelina away to his bedroom. Her mother collapses at the kitchen table and covers her ears. She mixes sobbing with reciting prayers to muffle the cries for help from her child. Later that evening, Evelina's mother teaches her daughter the lesson of survival as a house slave.

"Out in the field, you're whipped, beaten, and killed if you don't do what Massah says. That's because he owns your body like the Lord. But we got to do more for Massah than just work, 'cause he owns both our bodies and our minds."

The girl stares wide-eyed at her mother as she continues. "Evelina, you've got to figure out what he wants and who he wants you to be, and *do* it, *be* it for him—before he even asks for it! Put Massah's will above the Lord's will and let him consume your soul, for he can destroy you with a frown and a wave of his hand, just like the Almighty."

Thanks to Andrew Johnson and Evelina, the lineage of the mixed-race Johnsons began, or continued, keeping the paternal name even after Emancipation as was the case for most mixed-race house slaves.

Evelina had a son by Andrew Johnson, Lynier Miles Johnson, who fathered my maternal great-grandmother—Hattie Johnson.

The Johnson name and racial mixing, probably starting long before Evelina, led to more and more Caucasian genetics and genetic defects that ultimately doomed the house slave caste to extinction, not unlike the pharaohs of ancient Egypt. The interbreeding was by choice, by rape, or by arranged marriages to one's own fair-skinned half-siblings and close cousins on the same or neighboring plantations. The mulatto caste would continue to almost exclusively interbreed for another century after Emancipation.

Soon, congenital deformities, childhood diseases, and infertility beset the entire Johnson lineage. My mother became the only Johnson heiress four generations later; she had four childless maternal aunts and uncles, and a fifth one who produced only one daughter who died in her thirties from complications of juvenile-onset diabetes and vascular aneurysms.

My maternal great-grandmother had a stark, almost paper-white color, accentuated by her jet-black hair.

My Maternal Great-Grandmother
Her maiden name was Hattie Johnson.
She was the presumed granddaughter of President Andrew Johnson.

Her daughter, my maternal grandmother, Evelyn Johnson Foster, had four siblings and grew up well off—at least in comparison to other Negro families of her generation. She and her siblings could all almost pass as white, and often did so, when it was necessary for an advantageous survival with special favors.

A caste system based on "shades-of-color" was created in slavery. Originally, this was used to separate the two types of slaves from communicating household secrets or collaborating in a conspiracy against their masters, but later the caste system severely affected their freed offspring. This hierarchy was carried onwards, wherein mixed-race descendants, the "high yellow" minority of African-Americans, inherited a shallow sense of self-worth based merely on one's degree of whiteness.

My grandmother was eccentric and spoiled. She was used to living in a grand house and having darker-complexioned servants waiting on her. She could not cope with the poverty her proud, but underpaid, husband forced upon her. Her own income as a French teacher and an accountant did not bring in much money—it *was* the Great Depression.

Grandma was a flirtatious débutante, and then a vivacious socialite, who limited herself to superficial conversations and social niceties. After marriage, she became ensconced in nostalgic fantasies filled with fiction and mystery novels, music and 1920's dance steps. I remember her disinhibited pleasure, showing me how to dance the fast-paced kicking Charleston, the acrobatic feats of the Jitterbug, and the feverish shaking of the Shimmy. Grandma found that by being dissociated, she didn't have to feel bad about her poverty. She would sweep household dirt into a corner, cover it with a box, and then forget about its existence. As the years marched on, she inhabited a dream world to an extreme and her last years were plagued with Alzheimer's.

My grandmother had many phobias. She was very fair-skinned, virtually white, and had married a dark-complexioned husband who she dearly loved. Nevertheless, she had an issue about dark things. Pepper was *most certainly not* allowed on her food. She carried a white purse well stocked with sani-wipes, tissue, Lysol, disposable plastic gloves and spare pairs of white kid gloves, and a collapsible fly swatter. Flies were bigger and darker and worse than pepper. Once, she told me she had nightmares of someone stealing her obligatory purse. I wondered if the dream was an allusion to being raped by a dark-complexioned black man.

Touching pets was absolute taboo and they were quarantined from her. "They have black fleas," she fretted. She kept her clean cookware in a refrigerator with scarcely room for food. She always wore white gloves in public, which allowed her to collect change without having to touch it. "The coins have black germs on them!"

Evelyn Foster Holloway
My maternal grandmother
In a typical moment of dissociated leisure

Sometimes, my grandmother would invite guests from the University to come over for dinner. My mother is four years old, sitting up properly and ready to dip her spoon in her bowl of thick soup, following the rules of perfect etiquette that she had been taught. She is hungry; there hasn't been much food lately. Just then, a house fly falls into her bowl and is swimming around tenaciously. My mother doesn't know the right thing to do.

She whispers to Grandma, who is sitting next to her, "Ma, look. There's a *fly* in my soup." She points to her bowl.

Grandma is irked and snaps back curtly, in a way such that the guests won't hear, "No, there isn't! *Just eat it!*" My mother feels nauseated as she obediently spoons up the fly and gulps it down. Then she faints.

MY MOTHER
THE CHILD PRODIGY

Estelle Marie Holloway, my mother, was an only child and a lonely child; under strange circumstances, her parents abruptly left Nashville before she was born, to take up residence in a "teacher's cottage" in the woods of North Carolina. There, my mother lived an insulated life with no contact with other children and rarely any adults until she was seven. My grandmother had never learned to cook or clean; so, by age six my mother started sweeping, mopping, and cooking for her parents. But she had a great many *other* responsibilities to fill her childhood days.

My grandfather placed outrageous expectations on his daughter from an early age. Grandpa Holloway had an agenda for his only offspring: to *prove* his worth to the world that had looked down on him. He wanted to make his daughter a *prodigy*. He demanded that she assume the hefty responsibilities of being a role model for white society and "the best" at everything, without exceptions. She was to get right to the finish line first, under any or all types of necessary pressure, becoming a marvelous object that her father could show off to the world. He didn't *care* if the process would psychically undermine and pillage his daughter's individuality.

Mom lived in constant terror of her father's disapproval. Under his tyrannical rule, she felt a constant urgency to make him feel proud in addition to trying to placate him. Even as a one-year-old, she knew her survival and her safety depended upon gratifying his wishes. Complicating her situation even further was the knowledge that she had nobody else to whom to turn.

Meanwhile, her mother was lost in her dream world of pleasure and privilege, and offered little protection or guidance for her daughter, beyond providing her with some extra books to read and teaching the rules of social etiquette.

Estelle Marie was taught that to be a "child" was unacceptable, and she'd best snap out of it. The only useful elements of childhood to be retained were obedience and subservience to parental orders. My mother had to dispense with the rudiments of "growing up," forsaking any joyous pleasures of childhood and the camaraderie of peers. Thus, she became precociously studious, serious, and responsible.

Besides, there was nobody to play *with* or to even teach her *how* to play. She spent her first seven years living in the isolated teacher's cottage. Then the family returned to the homeland turf of Nashville, but she was not allowed to mix with any other children in the neighborhood.

Grandpa had decided that his child did not need school. He didn't even have to home-school my mother because she would learn by herself and by implicit mandates. She was handed novels, textbooks, and orders, with the subtle message that she must excel without coaching.

Thus, my mother was quarantined at home during these first ten years of critical psychosocial development, under the strict tutelage of her father's commandments. She was sequestered within the confines of familiar walls and zealously protected from the ordinary world outside. There would be no risk of contaminating her circumscribed life with *any* outside interference.

At age four, Mom began to read and write, as well as to practice playing the piano for four hours every day. By five, she learned to speak French. In the next years, she understood her parents' intellectual dinner table conversations, absorbed advanced mathematics, and became an excellent pianist.

By age ten, my mother had attained college-entry level skills and had become a piano virtuoso.

Perhaps by accident, or because of a concerned neighbor, the authorities were informed of my mother's hidden existence. She was immediately ordered to attend public school. Grandpa was incensed. To keep Estelle Marie out of the clutches of the public-school system, he demanded that she be tested. She was indeed scholastically at or near the college level. The educators were confounded. In the end, they decided to place her in the 10th grade of high school.

I imagine my mother's arrival for entrance to Pearl High School...

On the first day of school, Grandpa Holloway marches behind my ten-year-old mother into the large building. It is the first time she's ever been inside the walls of a school. She struts without prodding down the long corridors to the registration office. She looks grim, biting her lower lip to keep silent. Her father looms behind her at the counter.

"Are you *sure* that she's ready to skip *six* years, Professor Holloway?"

"Of course! How *dare* you question her eligibility?" Grandpa can barely contain his indignant pride. "Here's the letter!"

The principal and other school officials look at the report from the Board of Education. Then they look at the little girl. They are clearly amazed.

"My daughter can out-perform *all* of your students and I want her enrolled in only honors classes," demands Grandpa Holloway. *"You'll see!"*

My mother stands in stoical silence with perfect posture and a blank stare. Nobody would guess that she's secretly terrified or notice that she's scarcely breathing. They do notice, though, that she immediately soars to the top of her class.

She'll get accustomed to being stared at, treated as a "misfit," marginalized as a "loner," and envied as a "prodigy." For the next seven years, she will not participate in gossip, she will not be invited to parties, and she will never be allowed to have dates like the other young ladies. Her classmates were all adolescents going through puberty; the oddball brainiac who existed outside of their exclusive coterie only amused them. My mother simply did not fit in.

Just like living in the woods of North Carolina, or confined inside the home in Nashville, Mom was once again lonely and deprived of critical peer-bonding and the age-appropriate lessons of social skills. Estelle Marie would feel lonely and isolated for most of her life.

If Mom had any thought that by excelling she might cure her father's depression, she was wrong. Many years later, she would write in her journal: "I was born, a cherished offspring to fulfill a great destiny. So my parents thought, and so thought I, as I grew feeling the sperm of greatness like a sore in my heart and abdomen. Some incredible luck and outer force seemed to drive me on to conquer, easily, without obvious effort, but with tremendous emotional stress and strain, the difficult and almost impossible."

Estelle Marie Holloway
My mother
She is four years old in this photograph.

Long before Mom entered her adolescence, her father demanded more than *academic genius*. He also demanded *moral perfection*. His own father had been a preacher, so he believed he was passing on a tradition. Perfection alone was acceptable. She had to both achieve and behave…flawlessly.

My mother told me that when she was ten years old, she cheated on a French exam. She had never cheated before. There were twenty questions and she was not completely sure about one of them. Her classmate's test paper was very close, right under her nose. She tried to *not* look, but in a lapse of self-control, she saw the other girl's answer to the question in doubt and copied it.

Instantly afterwards, my mother was appalled at what she had done. Overcome with self-loathing, she wondered what Grandpa would say if he knew? There was the only solution: *She had to punish herself!*

She erased all her test answers and turned in a blank sheet to get the "F" she deserved. Later at home, she went to her room, closed the door, and cried tears of guilt and remorse. Then she found a sharp sewing needle. With furious self-hatred, she stabbed the hand that had cheated, piercing herself twenty times. *Twenty*—to atone for the twenty questions on the exam…

Mom easily excelled as a straight-A student and was unchallenged at the top of her class. But she graduated "second." She would have been the valedictorian, except for the fact that just before graduation one teacher changed her grade—refusing to give a "little girl" the 'A' she had earned. The teacher hated Grandpa for his arrogance and for what he'd done to his daughter, but claimed her objection was based on principles of "moral decency." The valedictorian was *eighteen* years old, and my mother was *twelve*.

She finished college at sixteen—*suma cum laude* and Phi Beta Kappa. Then, she received a scholarship to study mathematics at the University of Michigan, where she earned a master's degree in a single year. At seventeen, she was working as a college math professor, teaching students who were eight to ten years older than her.

But Mom loved piano more than *anything*. It was her passion and her dream. Her father could see how much she loved music and how gifted she was, endowed with an impeccable and perfect ear. It was rumored that she was one of the best emerging pianists in the country at the age of sixteen. She gave solo concerts in music halls and she ardently wanted to be a *performing* pianist. She begged her father to let her continue performing. But Grandpa was imperiously outraged at the thought.

He had decided that a career in the performing arts would take his daughter to strange cities where she would meet unsupervised men and become exposed to temptations. That was the stated motive behind his peremptory decision to force her to *stop* her burgeoning music career, and become a math teacher, like himself, instead. In that moment, my mother's tiny bit of adolescent freedom was crushed. Her spirit was pushed *underground* and out of the way. She had lost a sense of free will that would never be regained.

Grandfather was probably not consciously *concerned* that his image of a perfect daughter was merely a construct based on his own tortured past, or that the programming he would impart would replicate his own frustrated psyche, passed on for over six generations. He may not have *realized* that his daughter would then exist as his house slave, an extension of his ego, designed to service and gratify him and be chained to him forevermore.

My mother upon graduation from college at age 16

My mother was to behave as an impeccable and desirable débutante—except no boyfriends allowed. When she was seventeen, about the same time when she was forced to give up her career as a performing artist, she finally obtained permission for a date with a young man of acceptable class and social stature.

But when Grandpa saw her receive a sweet good-bye kiss from the boy as they lingered on his front porch, he was infuriated. What he saw was an indication of promiscuity! His draconian punishment was swift and trenchant. He refused to say a single word to his daughter for two entire years.

Marriage, with or without romance, was soon to come.

It was what was expected of her.

It was safer than dating.

After my father returned from Japan at the end of World War II, money from the GI Bill paved his way into the all-black Meharry Medical School. During his second year, his medical statistics teacher was Estelle Marie Holloway, a pretty girl, surprisingly young to teach, but just right to be his wife.

MY FATHER
THE MIXED-RACE ORPHAN

The year is 1926. The place is the home of Mrs. Mary Frances King of Glen Allen, Virginia—a hamlet outside of Richmond, Virginia. She is an elderly, fair-skinned, bourgeois-class black woman who, being childless herself, has graciously chosen to raise mixed-race orphans. Two such children currently live in her house, ages fifteen and six. Twelve have already grown up and left.

Mrs. King's doorbell rings and she opens her front door. On the doorstep, she finds my newborn father in a basket. The baby appears to be half awake and very still. In the basket, there is a hand-written note consisting of two sentences: The baby's name is Roy. He was born on April 20th.

Along with the note are instructions about a bank account, opened in Mrs. King's name, which will provide enough money to raise the orphaned child for many years. The infant is wrapped in a blanket marked "Coney Island Hospital."

This is *all* that my father would know about his ancestry for the next eighty years, when two wondrous things would happen. First, chromosomal genetic analysis will become available, thanks to both a web-based genetic analysis service and Y-chromosome studies at Stanford University, where my brother is a key researcher. Second, my father will receive a requested copy of his original birth certificate, but *two* certificates will arrive in the mail—one of them, done in accordance with the law, has the real parents' names blacked out. The other birth certificate, by sheer oversight, reveals two names: Eleanor Coleman and Morris Ginsberg.

Fifteen-year-old Eleanor Coleman is a mulatto who is part Native American, part African-American, and twenty percent Jewish. She accompanies her mother in search of temporary summer-time work in the North. They leave Virginia to go to the Catskills resort region of New York State, where her mother becomes the maid for the Ginsbergs, a wealthy Russian-Jewish family. A nineteen-year-old male member of that family, Morris, takes a special interest in the girl— he impregnates her.

Perhaps feeling something between shame and love, Morris Ginsberg chaperoned Eleanor's pregnancy and delivery of the baby at Coney Island Hospital. In *shame*, my father was to become an orphan; in *love*, he would be financially taken care of. In *shame*, he would never know a significant parental bond; in *love*, he would become a good financial provider for his family's physical needs, and a hard-working physician.

Roy Johnson King, MD
My father

So, my father, "Roy," grew up in a small foster home in a rural area outside of Richmond, Virginia. The caregiver, Mrs. King, from which my surname derives, was old, in poor health, and reluctant to take on her last abandoned child. She had dutifully and religiously raised her many prior foster children in a serious, joyless, manner. My father was eight when Mrs. King passed away. Roy was placed in another foster home, on a nearby farm run by Mrs. Johnson, Mrs. King's sister.

Dad's foster fathers were completely unavailable in both homes, being both physically and emotionally absent from both domestic life and childrearing. Dad cannot even remember his first "father." The second sealed himself away, mute and muted, in a carpentry shack on the farm and barely related to either my father or his domineering wife.

So, the burden of late childrearing fell on his second adoptive mother's tough shoulders, along with her harsh "work and don't waste time talking or feeling" farm philosophy. She got money for housing and feeding young Roy, but retained most of it for herself, making him earn his keep by hard work. The result was that my father became a relentless workaholic who felt useful, without learning to receive love or support.

If trauma can be genetically inherited, *then* my father would carry the *additional* burden of centuries of the Jewish history of slavery and oppression. But being an orphan was sufficient shame just by itself. My father's only self-esteem was based on a superficial sense of superiority above his adolescent peers. First, he was admired for his "whiter" appearance than most of the townsfolk. He was also smarter than almost everybody else in the small town where he grew up. He survived using his gift of public speaking to be the center of attention, and his garrulous humor to entertain his teenage peers. He was respected, but he did not make friends.

Like many orphans deprived of devoted parental attention, Dad was competitive and, like my grandfather, he was driven to achieve and prove his worthiness as "*better* than white." Dad was under-stimulated and bored, a "big fish in a little pond." So, he invented mind games to pass away hours of solitary farm labor and drudgery. He became valedictorian of his high school class, Virginia Randolph High School. Ninety-seven percent of his graduating class went on to college—*colored-only* colleges, of course.

*

And so, it happened that a mixed-race orphan who had never known a stable parent-child emotional bond or peer-group equals, and who possessed a self-centered egotism, was married to a child prodigy who had never had a childhood or peer contact, and suffered from a massively overbearing conscience. They would soon begin to raise two boys: Roy, Junior—and then, two years later, me.

In 1957, my father will take his family far away from the last remnants of social support my mother had ever known, away from everything familiar to her. With two sons—ages three and five—they will arrive in a new city as the first black professional couple, a doctor and a college math professor. They will soon become the *patriarch and matriarch*, the suburban de-segregationists, and the role models for an entire community. My family was destined to be a symbol of social status for 22,000 blacks and recent eastern European immigrants in a northern city of 220,000.

All four of us will be under a perpetual and jaundiced spotlight. All four of us must achieve and behave, flawlessly. We will be scrutinized, photographed, harassed, and taunted. We will face traumas and fight many battles. As you will soon see, we will be tested in many, many ways.

My fate was to live in an all-white world. I would barely even see another person of color outside of my own family from age six to fifteen. My destiny was to desegregate the "best" school systems in Erie, Pennsylvania as the first and only non-white student, in school after school. I was to carry the stigmata of both house slaves and field slaves—a house slave at home, in terror of my engulfing mother, and a field slave outside, in terror of violent whites.

I learned that my mother sincerely wanted me to fit in socially. She wanted me to have a better life than she had, one with peer contact and friendships. But I could not *both* achieve and behave flawlessly, and *still* fit into the world to which I was taken. Being black, I could not fit in socially, no matter *what* I did.

Perhaps the definition of "hero" is someone who *had* to and *could* do the impossible.

I did achieve.

We all achieved.

None of us ever fit in.

Perhaps my nephews will be free, accepted and loved at last.

CHRISTIAN DESEGREGATION

This narrative in three parts depicts both the struggle to desegregate the religious community in a conservative North Mid-western city in the late 1950's, and has many elements of direct and indirect child abuse.

The second short narrative represents the hallmark of child abuse and childhood trauma, racism and desegregation, and the first level of psychological defense against shame: dissociation. The third part is a seminal piece that captures all the elements of what is the basis of psychobiological oppression—a state that I call "toxic shame."

PART ONE: ERIE, PENSYLVANIA

Erie...

The most lucrative business, attracting thousands of workers, was General Electric. The plant was making all the components for nuclear missiles, from the electronic software to the shell and warhead. The community was told that the radioactive combustibles were made "elsewhere." We were also told that espionage had found a list of the ten top places to be annihilated first in a nuclear war with the Russians; Erie was high up on the list. Quite a few patriotic residents were proud of the city's lofty status.

Erie...

The headquarters of Hammermill Paper Company dumped millions of gallons of toxic waste into Lake Erie, until its brackish color and dead fish made the thought of swimming in the water both dreadful and hazardous.

I walk into the water from a beach on Presque Isle State Park with grave parental caution. "Don't let the water touch your face or enter your mouth." I see a dead fish with an eel attached, sucking its guts out. Some dense waterweeds wrap around my ankles, arms, and hands like slimy rope. Panic overcomes me as I run to the shore for safety in my mother's arms. When Hammermill employees had a weeklong strike, the water changed color from black to blue.

We moved to Erie in 1957 when I was barely three years old.
That's when my childhood amnesia stopped, and I began to remember.

*

PART TWO: THE BIBLE

I am sleeping on my bed loaned from the hospital, with the bars raised up to keep me from falling. It's my little cage of security. My five-year-old brother is asleep in his bed beside me. We share a small room in the modest three-room, third-floor apartment in the black and eastern European sector of town.

I awaken to the sound of my parents screaming outside the bedroom door. Suddenly, the door bursts open and light streams into the room, highlighting my brother's bed like a flash of lightning. In an iconic instant, I see my mother's tear-streaked face. Her right arm is raised up and back like a pitcher. She hurls a heavy black book at my brother's head. He bolts up, bawling. My father grabs my mother's arm and yanks her away from the door. The door slams shut.

I cannot cry. It is as if a hand were choking my throat. I cannot feel. My body and skin are numb. I do not understand why this has happened, but my Eden is shattered. I do not have any concept of God, or indeed of any benevolent entity except my mother and father, and they have now become acutely frightening to me. My mind then becomes blank. I have dissociated deep into my psyche.

This is my first conscious recall of shame and my first indelibly recorded memory.

Years later, I will learn that the book my mother threw that night was the Holy Bible. The minister of the First Baptist Church of Erie, Pennsylvania had interviewed my parents in the apartment earlier that day. They were the first Negroes to ever apply for membership in the all-white church. During the interview, my brother had been a bit rambunctious and embarrassed my mother who feared that the quest for desegregation had been lost.

Many years later, I realized that I survived this early phase of life by living in an elaborate fantasy world. It started with childhood amnesia, then talking to my toys instead of my parents, and ending ensconced in the make-believe world of adventure novels—"The Hardy Boys" and the "Tom Swift" series, or books by Isaac Asimov and Alfred Hitchcock.

Every weekend, I assembled model cars, submarines, and sailing ships, with little men on board that I painted and spoke to as if they were my friends. They were my token substitutes for real love. The models' fumes intoxicated me, and the smell of paint and glue kept intruders out.

*

PART THREE: CHURCH DAY

I'm seven years old. It's Sunday—Church Day. The smell of coffee and palpable tension percolates through the rushed breakfast ritual of Dad's waffles and bacon.

"Hurry, we must not be late for church!" Dad repeats, nervously. Mom urges me to dress as fast as possible. She helps me put on my Sunday suit and white shirt that I've outgrown. She buttons the collar; it feels uncomfortably tight around my neck.

Then we, the Kings, embark upon the silent, frantic drive to the First Baptist Church of Erie, Pennsylvania. Fear ripples through my tremulous limbs as we climb the stairs to the second-floor chapel foyer. We must stay close together! We represent a family, a good and decent family of four impeccable and correct social beings on a mission.

I try to stay glued to my parents and dare not stray, but my parents shift erratically to exchange pleasantries with strategic allies. I momentarily lose sight of my mother, who is blocked from view by the grown-ups, and I breathlessly squeeze my way through the converging throng of churchgoers in a desperate search for her.

We are a pack, a unit of one—*a good black Christian family.*

The chapel doors open and the organ plays the familiar signal that the *first* test has begun. The attendees move into the formation of two lines and prepare for the greeting by Reverend Emmons and the ushers that flank the doorways. Slowly, unbelievably slowly, we approach the portal, guarded by the two Sphinxes on either side. We are always in the line that must pass Reverend Emmons. He's the boss.

"What should I *say* to him, Mom?" My screechy voice betrays my trepidation. I rehearse the lines my mother tells me to say.

My hands want to hide in my pockets, but my mother has sewn all my pockets shut to prevent it. "It doesn't look good to put your hands in your pockets," she told me. She leans down to make sure my suit is not wrinkled, inspects my hair and face, adjusts my bow tie so it is rectilinear, and then pulls my collar to make sure the top button is not loose. I choke.

We're next!

My breath stops. I must extend my hand out to Reverend Emmons. He will grasp it firmly in both of his big hands and look me in the eyes. Will he see dirt on my brown hand? What is he looking for in my eyes? Can he see my sins? I must be allowed inside the cavernous temple where I will soon be baptized in the sunken pool behind the curtains— with the fear of drowning.

I arrive at the pew with relief. The backs of the mahogany benches are taller than my head and offer shelter. The *second* test begins: I must be as quiet and still as possible and I must not fall asleep for the next ninety minutes.

I imagine the treat at the end of the sermon; tea and juice will be served in the basement sanctuary and my mother will allow me one cup of tea, with lots of milk and sugar. I don't like the juice, but I always drink a cup to please the servers. The grapefruit juice is too bitter and the orange juice is too tart. They upset my nervous stomach.

The church ritual involves standing up and sitting down many times. My mother has a wonderful voice and sings with perfect pitch. I try to listen and follow her, but my voice is weak and I cannot hold enough breath for a whole line.

Eventually, Reverend Emmons starts his sermon. Although a Northern Baptist, he has the quality of a fire-and-brimstone style preacher whose words I do not understand: 'Sin, blasphemy, atonement, repent!' The crescendo and decrescendo of his droning and shouting soon put me in a trance. He begins to lurch over the pulpit toward the middle of his sermon, glaring at individuals in the congregation. I crouch down to hide behind the back of the bench in front of me.

The harangue seems interminable. I whisper to my mother, "How much longer, Mom?"

"Don't fidget!"

"Don't yawn!"

"Close your mouth!"

"Shhh! Be quiet!"

"Sit up straight!"

"LET US PRAY!" bellows the reverend. I push my spine still and stiff against the hard back of the wooden bench and bow my head. An invisible weight pulls my eyes down and my head is locked in place by the taut muscles of my neck. I look at my feet, which appear hazy and barely touch the carpeted floor. Then I am reminded to close my eyes.

I am now blind in the myopic darkness of the space behind my sealed eyelids. I do not inhale, I do not feel, I am not even here. Suddenly, I dissociate completely. I see myself from above, floating in the dense, hot air of the breezeless enclosed space of the enormous chapel. The words of prayer are coming into my head without comprehending. I just sense and know that I am *not* good, and that someone who is *not* Reverend Emmons sees me.

The pastor begins to pound the pulpit with his fists. I am startled from my reveries and look at him. I see froth coming out of the corners of his mouth and his hair has become disheveled from the furious jerking of his head. When the pounding gets louder, and reaches its feverish peak, it's a sign that: THE END IS NEAR.

Soon I will go down to the hot basement, sip on my saccharin-sweet tea, and mix it with bitter juice. Afterwards, we will go to the little store where my father will buy cigarettes, my mother will buy the Sunday paper reeking of freshly inked newsprint, and I will choose several comic books.

Then we will go for our traditional Sunday drive and I'll be sandwiched between my parents on the wide front bench seat of the Buick. We will look at the houses of rich people in the segregated *upper-class* neighborhoods. My father points at a plantation-style mansion and says, "You'll have a house like that someday, Michael."

He will not say that to my nine-year-old brother, who is studying a textbook on Calculus, sitting quiet and alone on the back seat.

And then I will then feel carsick reading *Superman*, nauseated by Dad's abrupt accelerations and decelerations of the car, by the smell of cigarettes and ink, and with my collar tight around my neck, which my mother will not unbutton.

This series of memoirs about being a solo child desegregationist in a hostile racist setting spans my developmental years from age five to fourteen.

UNCLEAN

My mother has decided that it would be a good idea for me to take swimming lessons at the YMCA, especially on Saturdays, so she could spend more time preparing lectures and grading exams for her university students. My parents inquired if Negroes could join and were told that I would be the first one in the beginner's class and it would be OK, if I behaved myself.

The ritual begins. My mother or father is usually rushed as they drive me downtown to the Erie YMCA, where they drop me off on the curb outside. A sinking feeling enters my body as their car speeds off, leaving me abandoned on my two skinny, shaky legs.

I walk up the stairs to the entrance of the dark multi-storied building that is infused with the strong smell of chlorine. I must be on time for the class or else I will not be allowed to participate. Instead, I would be stranded in the upstairs lobby, where the grownups would just stare at me for a couple of hours until my parents returned to pick me up.

I hurry downstairs to the basement where the big, cold swimming pool is located. The rule is that every child must strip, shower under ice-cold water using the antiseptic soap in the dispensers, and then line up naked at the pool's edge exactly on time.

Frequent shouts from the coaches exhort, "Hurry up! The class is about to start!"

I'm always on time. I wash my body thoroughly with the soap. I scurry out of the shower bay with the other boys. Then a whistle blow indicates: 'Last call!'

I line up for the first test: The "cleanliness inspection." I do not understand the meaning of the words, 'dirty nigger boy,' when I hear them whispered from the coaches, benches, and bleachers. But I feel eyes glaring at my nude body as I leave the shower bay.

The examiner is a middle-aged man. He scowls at me and gruffly grabs my two little hands and rubs them hard together. Then he shouts for all to hear, "You're still dirty! Go back and shower again!" There's laughter from the bleachers.

I am sent back to clean off invisible filth usually five or six times. Each shower leaves me feeling more rushed and panicky. The white boys never get sent back to the showers. I am increasingly breathless, trembling, dizzy, and weak after each failed cleanliness inspection.

Echoes of happy, shouting boys resound from the subterranean cavern of the huge pool chamber into the shower bay where I scrub my skin until it hurts. The "clean" boys are allowed playtime in the water before the instruction begins, while I try to scour the brown color off my skin.

The class instruction is always half over when I am finally allowed into the water. Without having the instruction or practice, I must proceed directly to the "swimming test" phase of the class. My skinny, bony body has no buoyancy. My limbs are too stiff and weak from shame to effectively kick or stroke; they flail awkwardly and without coordination in the ice-cold water.

I gasp for air as I struggle to swim the entire length of the endlessly long pool. Instead of air, water enters my frozen lungs. I reach up to grab the edge of the pool so I won't drown, but my arm and head are shoved back down into the deep end with the thunderous order, muffled by the water over my ears....

"KEEP SWIMMING!"

I gag and choke as my lungs fill with chlorinated water.

A PETRIFIED DRUMBEAT IS POUNDING INSIDE MY CHEST

I never passed the second test. I still have nightmares about being naked in lugubrious, cavernous buildings with shower stalls and a faceless audience on bleachers beside an underground pool—*smelling of sulfur instead of chlorine.*

The entire experience of solo child desegregation, which has not been addressed in literature before, is chronicled in a collation of vital segments.

BLEMISHED

It's 1960. My arrival at McKean Elementary School, and to the remote farmland countryside outside of Erie, Pennsylvania, was like a movie scene in which Whoopi Goldberg plays a scientist who is accidentally sent back in time to England during the reign of King Arthur's Court. She awakens with a mounted knight's long lance poking her, shouting, "Ogress!" Then she is prodded and paraded through the main street of the village and into the castle before the repulsed eyes of hundreds of onlookers who line up to gawk at her black skin, facial features, and dreadlocks.

Over the course of the next nine years, I will not be able to see or associate with other people of color outside of my immediate family. I will follow my parents as they desegregate one community after another, as they nudge their way up the socioeconomic ladder against increasing racist resistance— and always being "the first."

I would be the first non-white child to attend five different schools by ninth grade. Soon, with all-white role models, my mannerisms, speech, and perhaps my reality were indistinguishable from those of my white peers, except for one fact: To them, I was always an oddity and an outsider.

I'M AN OUTCAST.

*

I do all the rituals to try to look *not* black, but the nightly stocking cap ritual and avoiding the sun to stay as pale as possible doesn't work. *Nothing* works. To most of my peers, I'm still an ogre.

I'M HIDEOUS.

*

I would become the token representative for a whole race of human beings. My duty was to dispel negative preconceptions and stereotypes about blacks, and I was obligated to make an impeccable impression on all. The word "impeccable" stems from the Latin root, meaning "without a blemish," a "stain" or a "dark spot on the skin" that was interpreted in ancient times as a visible sin.

Sometimes I forgot that everybody was always watching me and waiting to see my visible sin.

I'M A SINNER.

*

My *first* day in *first* grade is an introduction to being the first one for much of the rest of my life. Nobody in the school, no teachers or students, had ever seen a non-white person before…or at least not live and close-up. For many, their only prior experience of colored people was on TV; they were usually denigrating caricatures such as on "The Three Stooges" or "Amos and Andy."

"Where are you *from*?" another six-year-old boy asks me.

"I'm from Hershey Road."

"NO, YOU'RE NOT!" he shouts. "You're from *Africa!* You're a *liar!* My daddy told me that you'd lie!" It's useless to argue the point with my classmate, and the formation of my social identity has begun.

I'M A LIAR.

*

I stand alone in a corner during the dreaded recess-time, watching the other children play ball, skip-rope, and hopscotch, laughing and shouting with excitement. I'm ashamed of my appearance; it prevents me from playing with my peers. I'm constantly teased and taunted. For Easter, most children bring in dark chocolate bunnies. At the lunch table, dozens of classmates point and snicker jeeringly at me as they bite off pieces of my voodoo bunny curse.

I have only one after-school white playmate by special arrangement and paid for by my father's influence, Jim Rhodes. My father gave the family free medical care in exchange for letting me have a friend, ten miles from home. One afternoon, I am watching the "Three Stooges" with Jim. A typical racist scene is depicting a black as hopelessly stupid and ugly. Jim's mother comes to the door and sees my little frozen body and blank stare at the TV. "Would you like to look at a *different* channel, Michael?" she immediately offers.

I am dissociated from all feelings and I am not even black at this moment. I lie. "Oh, no. It doesn't matter...." Then I feel the waves of agonizing shame and mortification sweep over me and tears stream down my cheeks. I look away and hide my face from Jim, who is still watching the show.

*

The summer before I enter 5th grade is when my family finally manages to move from the countryside to the suburbs of Erie—an upper-middle class area of the city. My homeroom teacher is Mrs. Sutton, who is derisively dubbed by my classmates: "Mrs. Sutton, the Old Fat Glutton."

I am in the cafeteria line. The two boys ahead of me have playfully dashed down to look under the skirt of a girl in front of us. The only rule of the game is to not get caught by either the girl or Mrs. Sutton. I am pressured and urged by my peers to follow suit or else be called a sissy. Reluctantly, I squat down and peek.

Mrs. Sutton has been watching the whole event and has been waiting for "my turn" the entire time. She ignores the other peepers. The extra-brutal spanking leaves me stinging and silent for many days. The other boys are just chastised. The message is vague but clear: "'I'm an over-sexed Negro craving white women."

I'M A BEAST.

*

The class is reading "Huckleberry Finn" and "Tom Sawyer." When the passages with the word "nigger" are read out loud, the skin of my face burns in flames of shame as every student turns around to stare at me. The worst part is that all my classmates have now also learned the word "nigger" and how it impales me.

I'M A SPECTACLE.

*

I'm in 8th grade. Now, whenever the words "Negro" or "black" or even "Africa" are mentioned in class, the students no longer turn and stare at me. At first, I feel relief and freedom from the heat of other's intense scrutiny. Then, slowly, I sense that something *worse*; something very ominous and sinister is beginning to occur.

I AM EFFACED.

*

Cold hatred is like a sister whose brother is *hot* hatred. Cold erasure is the wife who never ventures to see or even cares about the plight of the blacks across the railroad tracks; it's just where her servants disappear after curfew. Hot erasure is when her husband dons a white cloak and cylindrical cap and mounts a horse to visit the other side of the tracks, looking for an innocent young man to lynch. Being effaced can go either way.

*

The biggest challenge now becomes the complex issue of how to get to school and back home safely. Since our house is within walking distance from my brand-new junior high school, I have three options: to take the shortcut through the woods and enter the back doors of the school; to walk along six long blocks of paved sidewalk in front of the houses of dozens of neighbors; or to have one of my parents drive me to school and drop me off.

The path through the woods is physically *dangerous*, but has the advantage of avoiding the mingling crowd of kids at the main entrance as they wait for the doors to be unlocked. The front-entrance kids are unpredictable and cruel to me when no teacher is around. They won't talk to me and leave me isolated in a corner.

But the woods are the hiding place where the "naughty" kids hang out—smoking cigarettes, drinking beer, and acting tough. They're called the "Hoods" and usually come from lower working-class families and belong to gangs of bullies. They also carry army knives or pocketknives with bottle openers for their beer. Like switchblades, I can see the flash of razor-sharp metal, open and prepared.

The usual trick is to detect *them* before they can detect *me*. I walk through the woods from tree to tree, hyper-vigilant, ready to run or take a wide detour upon seeing the Hoods. I've learned to talk my way out of the rare times I am caught and encircled with knives and racial insults. I'd rehearse what to say and do for those confrontations. I was even prepared to use bribes and mind games.

I'M A NIGGER.

*

The sidewalk route offers physical safety, but I must endure a special *psychic torture* as I walk alone, past house after house. The housewives stand at their windows waiting to gawk at me. Generally, the staring is obvious: A white man is conspicuously standing guard in the dead middle of his front yard and territory, to make it clear that I and my family and my people do not belong in this upper-middle class neighborhood. I greet the neighbor, "Good morning, *Sir!*" I receive a hostile squint in response.

Sometimes it is *subtle*; out of the corner of my eye, I see the parting of a curtain with an anxious woman's face looking, but trying to not let me know she's looking. Nearly every house is like that. I can barely manage to move my legs. It's an ordeal like those nightmares when one is trying to move but can't; like trying to run through deep water or mud, or like the sleep paralysis of narcolepsy.

I'M A DISGRACE.

*

Asking one of my parents to drive me to school, when or if they have a moment, is the easiest, safest, and fastest method. I'm proud of my parents' money; we have one of the most impressive houses, one of the largest lots, and they always drive two of the flashiest, "model of the year" cars.

Dad drives me to the front door of the school building in his shiny sports car. This year, it's a brand-new red Buick GS455. Mom carries me in her brand-new Buick Electra 225. At first, it works.

Then, I begin noticing *new* stares, scowling and contemptuous stares, different from all the other stares, and more penetrating and hostile than the Hood's knives. A group of teachers is *looking down* at the car and me from the classroom windows above the main entrance. They are filled with venom toward my family's intrusion. It's always the same teachers, leaning into each other, smirking, gesticulating, and pointing at me. Their cold stares flagellate my facial skin like a whip.

'What are they plotting?' I wonder. I *look down* in dread.

Later I found out that I was a "hot topic" in almost every faculty meeting. Approximately one-third of the teachers persistently petitioned that I be expelled because I was "a *future* militant radical."

I'M A THREAT.

A critical encounter with the KKK and community violence, with my father's heroic courage, makes this excerpt an exceptional depiction of the horrors of desegregation.

THE CROSS

Part of the front of our house in Erie

I'm ten years old. It's summertime. I'm sleeping like an angel in my bedroom that faces the front yard and the street. My family is finally settled in our new home—a spectacular brick sanctuary for which my mother was the sole architect and designer, a long multi-angled ranch house with ten-feet-tall flush panes of glass for the front-facing sunken living room, a grand piano alcove, and a raised formal dining room.

Sunday outings after church always included a visit to the new homestead as it was being built. The colossal deep basement and the wood smelling of fresh pine enthralled me. I skipped from future room to room… "Is this going to be *my* room? All by myself?" I'd ask my mother over and over, standing in my wood-framed bedroom without walls. I looked out of my glassless window at the dirt that would soon be a carpet of rolled-out turf.

We attended our first neighborhood picnic in the new community called "Winchester Heights" and nothing untoward or shocking happened. I was on my very best behavior and even my brother was subdued and cautious. A few neighbors talked to us; most just looked and whispered among themselves.

It had been a struggle for well over a year to arrive in this all-white upper-middle class subdivision. My father tried to purchase the lot and deed to build in Winchester Heights, but the seller balked saying, "I can see you and your wife are good people and you have the cash to buy, but I can't let you build. If others see that a black family is living here, it will ruin future sales, *ruin me.*"

Finally, he relented with a compromise and a signed note that stated: "I will keep lot #1105 Greenfield Drive un-sold for ONE year at which time it will be sold exclusively to the family of Roy and Estelle King." *Exclusively!* And he kept his promise.

We bought the largest lot in the community and Dad could even practice golf in the back yard. But for me, the new lawn was the most magical event of all. One day a big truck arrived and I watched as perfect, dense green grass was rolled out in long strips to make an immaculate front lawn outside my window. Soon my father began to mow it on his special-made, triple-wide, seated lawn mower built like a mini-tractor.

An anecdote my father tells us at dinnertime makes us all feel victorious and proud. "Well, I was on the mower and this Cadillac stops on the street beside me. This old white man calls out, 'Hey, *BOY!* You there! Who owns this nice house?' So, I said, 'Yessah, uh … uh … Doctor King, *HE* own this here house, Sah!' Then the man orders, 'You *TELL* Doctor King I'm interested in buying this house!' Then he gave me his phone number."

Dad continues, "When I got to my office, I called him and said, 'Hello, Mr. Smith, this is *Doctor* King. We met when I was mowing my front lawn. I'm sorry, but we don't think you're the *right kind of people* for our neighborhood."

We all laugh hilariously. We've won the battle for desegregation and we all feel safe and victorious.

*

It's well past midnight. Abrupt sounds, loud sounds, and bright lights begin an insidious crescendo outside my bedroom window. Then I hear *pounding* sounds and I see a *blazing* light that appears just outside the window; immediately afterwards, I hear *THUMPING* sounds and *CRASHING* sounds and *SHATTERING* sounds of breaking glass. The strings of the Steinway grand piano twang and rip as rocks strike it. Pip, the German shepherd in the basement, is barking furiously.

I hold my breath, terrified, and listen to my parents in their bedroom. "No, Roy, NO! *Don't do it!*" I hear my mother pleading with my father. A drawer slams shut. "I've *got* to do it, Estelle. Let go of me!"

My bedroom door suddenly bangs open. My father has a World War II pistol in his hand. "GET UNDER YOUR BED, MICHAEL, RIGHT NOW!" my father commands through clenched teeth. In a twilight state of warped time and instant obedience, I am now crouching under my bed. I hear the dog running loose and in ferocious attack. I smell gasoline.

I am looking out my window at a large white wooden cross in orange flames with the silhouettes of hooded white-clad men dashing around it. The big cross is burning on the lovely, impeccable front lawn. It will be tainted with the huge burnt-out figure of the cross when it falls, like a brand on a Jew's forehead, like a blemish for all to see as they drive by the house for a long time.

My father sleeps with a rifle on the broken glass of the living room, waiting for "them" to come back. Eventually the windows are replaced. But there's no money to cut out and replace the burned stigma of the lawn for four eternal months of unimaginable disgrace.

This very short piece captures my mother's denial and unsupportive nonchalance about racial violence.

FROM A MILE AWAY

I am building a tree house with my brother and our tiny group of two white friends. It's a perfect tree, at the farthest edge of the expansion of our subdivision. It even has a stream running beside it.

Construction of new homes is underway nearby and we need some extra wood. I bravely take the lead and walk about a tenth of a mile away to where there appears to be a pile of discarded wood, and I call out to the carpenter who is working on the frame of a new house. "Hello, sir. We're building a tree house and we're a little short on wood. Do you have any you could spare?"

My earnest politeness pleases him and he points to the pile, giving me permission to take it. He wouldn't have to cart it off to the dump that way. Happily, I carry the wood over to the base of the tree in several long hauls. Hours later, in the fading evening light after sunset, I am still in the tree hammering away by myself.

Suddenly I hear a man yelling at me from another house under construction, "*YOU, nigger boy!*" I freeze, speechless. In the dim light, from a good distance, I can barely see the white man who is beginning to storm over toward me. He is now at the base of my tree.

His next words stop my heart and penetrate my head like a spear.

"You're a *thief!* You stole that wood! I'll make you *pay* for it!"

I climb to the top of the tree where he can't reach me. "No, sir. The man...who, who was there before...told me to...to...take it...OK?" I gasp.

"You're a *liar!* I'm going to make you *pay* for this!" He heads back to his construction site to get something. I know I must run away fast. I climb down the tree, sliding, slipping, and falling. My knee starts bleeding from a scrape. I run as fast as I can straight to my home a half-mile away, sobbing in terror. "Mom, the carpenter called me a nigger, but it was dark and far away."

"Michael," she says sternly, "white people can see the color of your skin from a *mile* away." My being so foolish as to imagine "passing" visibly irks my mother. She returns to her deskwork in stern silence without any words of consolation or comfort. I bandage my knee. There will be no tree house.

The following short trilogy focuses on my public-school experience, trying to both excel and fit in: Running for Office— Lunchtime— Shot Down Again...

RUNNING FOR OFFICE

I win the election to become the president of the Student Council in 9th grade. I do not win because of *popularity*—my rival is a beautiful blonde girl and head cheerleader. I win the campaign by *strategy*.

First I announce a "Poster Party" to produce scores of advertisements for my campaign on poster-sized paper. I offer each artist that comes to my house ten dollars, loads of pizza, and drinks. Is it bribery? Soon the walls of the school are covered with a hundred clever drawings and slogans like "KING FOR KING!"

Next I target the impressionable and easily swayed 7th grade kids by going into each homeroom to introduce myself and give a short speech. I ask the students what changes they'd like or want in the school. Like any politician, I make promises that I know I can't fulfill, such as more leisure time to "hang out in study hall," presumably to do their homework.

I know I already have name recognition. I have an easy name, often heard in the media as *"Martin Luther* King," and often overheard by me as my name is muttered on the lips of every student. "He's the black kid, you know, *the N….*"

I win by only a few ballots and the cheerleader becomes my vice-president. But nobody cares that I am now "the president." It doesn't change my social status in the least.

*

LUNCHTIME

I dread lunchtime in the school cafeteria as much as dinnertime at home. With a full tray in my hands, I scan the crowded room for a place to sit. But students move away, suddenly "finished eating." Some slide their trays to another seat, as if to chat with a friend, and thus avoid sitting next to me. Some block the seat with personal belongings as I approach, "Oh, I'm saving the seat for a friend." Or, "It's taken."

Nobody wants me to sit next to him or her. They're in cliques to which I don't belong, they're having closed conversations from which I'm excluded, or they just ignore me in intransigent silence because I'm the Black One. I have no choice but to sit alone and without friends, or at a table with the few other "rejects," usually slow learners from the special classes.

*

SHOT DOWN AGAIN, KING

I have a science teacher who hates me. He's an ex-drill sergeant from the army and he still acts the same. He's also one of those who watch me enter the building every morning, smoldering in envy and stewing in prejudice. I imagine his thoughts: 'It is not right that a black should be the smartest and one of the richest students in an all-white school.'

My only goal is to please the teacher and to learn. His goal is to humiliate and shame me with unmitigated and sadistic cruelty in front of my peers. I eagerly raise my hand to give the correct answer to his questions. He ignores me, but when nobody else raises his or her hand, he shouts, "OK, *KING*. So, what do *you* think is the answer?" Then he habitually and automatically shouts without explanation, no matter what answer I give, *"WRONG!"* My classmates love it, laughing at me. Then another student repeats exactly what I'd said and is told, *"RIGHT!"*

His harshest words, spoken to me every class-time over and over, are: *"SHOT DOWN AGAIN, KING!"* Martin Luther King has just been murdered and I hear the words in a different way than, perhaps, they are intended.

He intensifies his public scorn when I am accepted into private boarding school. "EXETER? *MISTER BIG SHOT!*" His thick snarl of scathing hatred becomes like that of a brutal leopard about to kill.

Another short piece that depicts a graphic extreme of racial violence perpetrated against a helpless child.

TENSION

American politics became a personal vulnerability for me in the 1960s. Race was now an incendiary issue due to shocking events that riveted the country. A bigoted backlash naturally targeted me as the visible "King"—the icon of climbing the social ladder over whites.

Students who I did not know would wait for me as I left a classroom just to say, "I *hate* you!" Shocked, I'd ask, "Why?"

They wouldn't tell me...

When I return to Erie on spring break during my first year away at Exeter, I decide to revisit my prior junior high school's guidance counselor. Gino Carlotti is an Italian-born immigrant and the most liberal adult in the whole school. He reminds me of the "Bikini Hop" dance I'd organized the previous year. It was a daring event where students were permitted to wear short pants to a school dance.

"You were so busy setting up the dance room that you forgot to wear the required shorts. Before you dashed home through the woods to change into your shorts, you told me the color and style of the shorts you'd wear when you came back—saying that's how I'd recognize you," Gino recalls.

He continues, "Michael, *everybody* recognized you! You stood out like a sore thumb. It didn't matter what color your shorts were. You were the only black kid we'd ever had! How could you have denied the obvious color of your skin, marking you for life?" As he guffaws, a deep, disturbing shame, sadness and rage sweep over me.

Then I reminisce about the Bikini Hop Dance night...

*

I feel awkward and alone, standing in a corner and watching the boys and girls dancing. I approach a few girls and ask to dance with them, only to be hastily turned away. Soon my skin feels hot and stinging from the rejections. I find a role as servant and pour Kool-Aid and Coca-Cola, and serve appetizers for the dancers.

I leave the school by the backdoor toward the end of the dance party. I am suddenly surrounded by over a dozen older thugs from the lower-class "Westlake High School," whose intentions are as clear as the boy in the driveway alley of my past. It was, perhaps, a preview of much later, when I will walk through a mass of murderers and thieves in the concrete yards of San Quentin Prison and I would think, *'Yea, though I walk through the valley of the shadow of death....'*

"**LOOK!** It's a nigger, and he's *all by himself,*" shouts a heavy-set thug.

"I'm *pleased* to meet you all!" I say cheerfully and calmly as they close in on me. I continue to act nonchalant.

"I'm the president of the Student Council here and I organized this dance." I must not look frightened. Now it's time for hypnotic suggestion and bribery. I only have a few moments left before being assaulted.

"I can open up the dances to *ALL OF YOU.* There are so many pretty girls inside. Would you like to get in for *FREE?*"

The thugs put their weapons and their hands back inside their coat pockets. I walk straight through the circle and then back myself into a blind corner of the building to take a deep breath.

MY HEART IS POUNDING TO THE FAST TAPPING OF TERROR.

Then I dash and *run for my life* through the familiar woods. In my panic, I hallucinate a ghastly Hood with a cigarette dangling from his snarling mouth, then another with an open switchblade flashing in his hand, then a *horde*, emerging like phantoms from behind tree after tree——each one muttering the same words with repulsion:

"NIGGER!"

"I HATE YOU!"

The drama of being alone and left to fight my own battles is amplified by my mother's hysteria and attempt to control my freedom.

ON MY OWN

I always felt acutely anxious, weak, and clumsy under the visual dissection of my disgusted peers who shunned me or taunted me with whispered, and sometimes loud, racial slurs. I only reported being called "nigger" once to my parents; it was easier to just quietly bare it. In fact, almost *all* the racial abuse I suffered was kept secret from my parents.

I'd tried to tell them once or twice about an incident, but my mother just blamed me. "What did *you* do wrong that warranted such punishment, Michael?" she queries. Or she'd tell me I was *foolish* to expect to be treated decently. I was black. End of story...

Or, she'd become hysterical, calling and screaming at the principal, while Dad called his "connections," until the whole incident was blown out of proportion and the repercussions were *not* good. Besides, my mother was far too fragile and unpredictable; I had good reason to fear that *my* tragedies, when added to *hers*, could lead to her death.

My parents just didn't understand. They *couldn't* understand how infinitely complex and politically delicate my whole developmental life was: I was "a solo child desegregationist." I've never met another black of that time whose experience was even close to mine.

I'm in mid-adolescence now, at the very end of 9th grade. I've finally had a few dates with a girl named "Ruth" from a liberal Lutheran family. She's a skinny, plain-looking girl with acne. But she *is* smart and she *is* the president of the Honor Society. It seems a logical match that the two class "presidents" should date. But the relationship is doomed from the start. I'm devastated when her neighbors who see us together threaten her parents and throw rocks at their property.

Since all but one of my white male peers had rejected me, I'd settled on a handful of Jewish boys who I *thought* were friends. My two most trusted Jewish peers tell me, "You must give Ruth to *one of us* because we're *whiter* than you are."

The betrayal of my Judases is followed by my mother's flat refusal to let me date any girl at all. Early in June, after 9th grade ended, I'd hoped to date Ruth like other boys who had girlfriends. My mother is outraged and snatches up a calendar to shove in my face as she bangs open my bedroom door. "You can see Ruth *four* times over this three-month summer break. Choose the days and mark them on this calendar, *right now!*" she demands.

My protests are useless. I feel hemmed in, defeated and angry. I've lost all trust; both my "friends" and my mother have destroyed my first relationship. Yet, given my mother's moralistic upbringing and her entrenched condemnation and disgust at non-marital sexual activity, it was not unexpected.

This valuable segment depicts my mother's breakdown and the most vicious racist attack on me as a fourteen-year-old, set up by my brother's betrayal. It segues into the beginnings of black political power centered in my family home.

DOUBLE JEOPARDY

My sweet obedient charm had served me well, at home as the sleeping angel and at school as the perfectly behaved and exceedingly polite student. It was possible to maintain sanity and function with a combination of major dissociation and hypervigilant diligence both at home and at school. In the late spring of 1968, however, a vast number of simultaneous events collided and converged into the worst single moment of my developmental years.

My older brother had been away at Exeter for almost two years, leaving me as the sole provider for my mother's emotional needs. Now, I, too, had been accepted to attend Exeter to try to follow my brother's footsteps. My mother was overwhelmed with grief, losing both her children at age fifteen.

Then a *coup de grâce* struck like a bolt of lightning, and my mother was soon to experience a "breaking point." She was finishing her belated doctorate and writing the dissertation, which was, of course, stressful enough. Toward the end of her graduate school requirements, she needed a copy of her original birth certificate for some obscure reason.

When it arrived, my mother "looked" at the recorded birthdate on the certificate, but at first she could not "see" it. Slowly the truth leaked out of the piece of paper and dripped like an intravenous infusion into her consciousness. She had been born on December 11th—*not in late February*. Suddenly she realized that she had been *conceived out-of-wedlock* and had been lied to by both her parents for forty years.

Now she knew the true reason behind the sudden move from Nashville to the remote woodlands outside of Greensboro, North Carolina immediately after her parent's marriage. And perhaps the real reason she'd been kept out of public schools; a birth certificate was only required for grade school entry, not for high school.

"CRACK*!" Fists pound the piano keys with such force that the strings break and the ivory keys snap loose.*

Grandpa Holloway, the stentorian and moralistic disciplinarian of her past, was a liar and a hypocrite! The violent strictness of her self-judgment—always striving to live up to his unattainable standards of behavioral perfection—turned into a wrenching and fully conscious loathing of her deceitful parents.

The core structure of her identity instantly collapsed. My mother fragmented into a breakdown lasting many long months, diagnosed as a state of psychotic depression. She lost control of her rage and inflicted horror on her husband and me, as well as upon herself. She became *Ophelia*, the Mad Woman, when given tranquillizers, alternating with the viciousness of *Medusa* when the medications wore off a bit.

She was confined to her bedroom and over-sedated by my father who virtually vanished from the home to escape her attacks—choosing to spend his intimate time "elsewhere." Mom's nonstop stream of suicidal threats and daily attempts, her screaming and ranting, her throwing knives and pointing scissors at anyone who came close to her would all be a partial haze in my tremulous recollection and nearly a total amnesia in hers.

"You go talk to your mother and calm her down, Michael. She'll *only* listen to you," my father orders, as he had ordered for years past and he will for many more years to come.

I could barely cope with my mother's tragedy when at home, such that the stress and trauma began to bleed over into my separate school-time struggle for survival. I had a haunting and terrible anxiety about whether I would find my mother *dead or alive* when I came home after school.

I suffered sleep deprivation from watching over her night after night. My conscious filter, which I depended on to suppress traumatic recall about dreadful scenarios at home, became unreliable and vivid, violent flashbacks intruded unpredictably into my psyche. It was becoming *very* difficult to maintain my persona, my sweet industrious façade, at school.

I had insulated my ego within the structure of "being perfect" at school. My academic record was unblemished and I was undeniably the best student in the junior high school of one thousand students. My behavior was impeccable. I was president of the student council, editor of the school newspaper, president of the debate club that I founded, and I'd even started a "hallway monitor system" to improve the behavior of *other* students, for which I was the purported role model.

My brother provided the next ingredient of the lethal concoction when he arrived home on his spring break from Exeter. His fiendish betrayal was as potent as hemlock was for Socrates.

Freed from constant shame and abuse at home, he'd quickly acquired new narcissistic defenses, bolstered by achieving notoriety at the prestigious academy as a math and science "superstar" and by his early acceptance from eleventh grade into the best mathematics program in the country. He was on a path to obtain a PhD in pure mathematics from Cornell University by age twenty-one. Now he felt invincible and his empathy, what little he still had of it after his years of abuse, was nowhere to be found.

Unknown to me until decades later, my brother went to visit my junior high school and talk to *his* former supporter—the *same* guidance counselor, Gino Carlotti. But the most racist teacher and white supremacist, Mrs. Butler, found out that my brother was in the building and rushed up to Roy, Junior. She had to ask him a loaded question: *"Is Michael a big problem at home, TOO?"*

My brother has a rare opportunity to avenge himself for being tattled on by me, for being darker complexioned, and for being my parents' favorite and obedient house slave child. He answers convincingly and matter-of-fact, "Well, *YES*, actually. *He really is a big problem at home!"*

My brother confirmed Mrs. Butler's basis for *HOT* hatred; I was a disobedient, arrogant, and ambitious rebel. I was the field slave who deserved a good whipping. My brother cleverly and effectively reversed the truth of our family dynamics; he happily betrayed me to a dangerous predator with a preposterous lie and would continue to do so for the rest of his life. That ill-fated day, all the spheres collided and I almost got stuck in a traumatic moment.

I am standing in the main hallway being a good student monitor, trying to hold back agonizing secrets about my last nights at home. Mom is getting worse, *much* worse. I see Mrs. Butler slowly approach walking down the long corridor in front of me. She's wearing coarse wool stockings—a proud relic of WW II—her usual black skirt, white blouse, and grey vest. Her silver hair is in a perfect bun. Her eyes are taut and intense, like ruby lasers penetrating me.

Old Mrs. Butler stops and stands still six inches in front of me. She is the same height as me in her thick high heel shoes. I greet her. In very slow, deliberate, and silent motion, she puts on her stark white gloves so that *her skin* will stay uncontaminated by touching *Negro skin*.

Then she starts to slap my face over and over, *LEFT*, *RIGHT*, as *HARD* and as *FAST* as she possibly can…until I collapse onto my knees in defenseless shock, fallen limp like prey in the jaws of a predator, in complete psychic surrender to death. When I regain some consciousness, I look up at my executioner and utter one feeble word: "Why?"

Mrs. Butler wears a triumphant smile as she briskly turns around and struts away, dusting off her gloves in imperious silence. I kneel, crying in front of a group of students who are enjoying the show.

Unlike my mother, I did not experience a breakdown.

Instead, I had a transition point to a *stronger* identity.

*

Did Mrs. Butler *also* attack me because Carl B. Stokes of Cleveland had just been a guest in our home, where my family hosted a reception during his 1967 campaign to become the first black mayor in the history of the United States?

Carl B. Stokes, America's first black mayor
"With his victory, the era of black political power had come of age."

Citation from article in About.com Cleveland Guide by Sandy Mitchell; 2010; originally from "Carl B. Stokes and the Rise of Black Political Power," Leonard N. Moore; University of Illinois Press; 2002

In 1972, it would be Shirley Chisholm who stays at our home during her presidential campaign.

Congresswoman Shirley Chisholm
The first black and the first woman to run for nomination by the Democratic Party in her bid for the Presidency…

There were many such parties, featuring black candidates and liberal local dignitaries, including the long-term mayor who always got drunk. It was well known that my family had as many protective connections as we had enemies. Mayor Tullio and the chief of police were supportive. Democrats downtown, but the suburbs where we lived were overwhelmingly Republican. My father had a tremendous influence on the voting patterns of the sizable black, Jewish, and eastern European immigrants who were his patients, and many more citizens who respected his reputation as "patriarch and spokesperson for the minority communities." But racial tensions only continued to mount for me—targeted as a mere child—and I had to fend for myself daily.

Soon I would leave my parents, my home, and Erie behind and scarcely ever return. I would also leave behind my innocent little sleeping angel subpersonality. Shifting into my own anger, I would be ready for the fierce academic competition ahead.

This humorous anecdote with elements of racism and xenophobia in gym class (9th grade) demonstrates my ardent ambition to achieve and please my mother... with a twist ending.

STRAIGHT A's

I am in my last few months of 9th grade, 1969. I've earned a reputation for being a skinny brainiac who isn't very gifted at athletics. I am a "Negro nerd." The nerds attend advanced honor's classes and the jocks do not. The jocks are popular and the nerds are not. The white jocks *and* the white nerds get to have girlfriends or at least an arranged escort, freedom to walk beside or dance with girls and go to parties—*and I do not*. I have never been invited to a party. I have never even been invited to a classmate's house, except for two Jewish families and a neighbor or two, in nine years.

I've also been excluded from team sports since elementary school. To almost always be the last player to be picked for a team is humiliating, especially when I'm openly referred to as "the nigger." So, I just stopped trying to play sports with my peers completely. The only experience of sports outside of school was when my father tossed a ball for me to practice batting. That happened for less than twenty minutes on one occasion when I was in 4th grade.

I feel uncomfortable with the gym teacher. He stares at me when I take my shower after class, but so do the other boys. What are they looking for? Do they still want to see if I clean myself? Are they looking at my hair, which begins to curl up in the steam into "not white"? But the stares are always *lower down* on my body.

Gym teachers don't need teaching credentials in 1969; like my science teacher, a military record and boot camp are apparently sufficient. My teacher is crude and uneducated; he's what I'd later learn is called a redneck.

He constantly yells and shouts and butchers up non-English immigrant names during roll call. He loves to intimidate and punish several students for half of each class hour for *any* reason whatsoever, but especially for being late for class. And he *especially* doesn't like kids with last names that he can't pronounce. They're usually the ones he loves to punish for being late.

'I've got to get there on time!'
'I've got to pass the tests!'

The teacher is adept at thinking up creative and sadistic ways to humiliate his favorite victims, to make the other students laugh and yell at the unfortunate ones like a mob before a pilgrim locked in the stocks. But the gym teacher does *not* know how to think up creative ways to teach athletic fitness.

No coaching, no training, no fun; just warm-up orders, then line up to be tested, one by one, in front of all the other students who stand watching and waiting for *their* turn to be tested. The number of sit-ups or push-ups you can do in two minutes or before collapsing; the number of successful basketball hoops out of ten trials; how high you could climb a rope in thirty seconds—the number is predetermined for everything. The grade you receive at the end of each quarter of the school year is simply the average of those numbers. And I have always gotten a B in the class, which is always my only non-A grade.

Deep inside, I do not want to get an **A** in gym. Blacks are *supposed* to get an *A* in gym because we are closer to apes from Africa than humans from Europe. Blacks are *supposed* to be in special classes for slow learners because of the same reason. My mission is to dispel stereotypes.

I hate gym class. But I *must* get an **A** in gym so that I can finally stand up in the auditorium when the straight-A students are honored. I want to bring Mom a report card and not have to feel ashamed to say once again, "Do you want to see my report card, Mom? I got an *A* in everything *except* gym."

The last quarter has two tests: gymnastics and high jump. I'm wiry and skinny; I know my *only* athletic advantage is over gravity. I know I can ace the gymnastics. I've done that before. But for the high jump I must practice. I also must overcome my fear of falling. So, I create a makeshift high jump bar in the backyard from tree branches and a metal beam. For cushioning, some blankets are all I need. I clear snow from a wide swatch of the lawn exposing the wet, slippery grass.

I'm willing to break my neck to get that **A**. I run and jump and fall for hours, until it's dark and I'm shivering in the cold snow, then drenched in the cold springtime rain. The second practice session, I break my thick black glasses. So, I practice without them; somehow the bar seems less scary that way. Being nearsighted and nearly blind, I begin to sense and learn by intuition where the bar is and when to jump. I scrape my knees on the bar. I bruise my back and shoulders and crash my skull hitting the ground like a madman.

Finally, the test day comes. "KING!" the gym teacher roars. My approach is at a perfect angle; I know just when to kick my left leg up, lift high in the air, twist my torso, and land safely. The teacher is shocked when I have only one rival student left. The bar is staggeringly high, higher than my head. My last chance to prove myself—*my battle to redeem the nerds!*

And I did it! I ace gym, completing what I set out to do. I'm ecstatic. I'm proud. I bring my report card home for Mom to see. "Mom, do you want to see my last report card?"

She's sitting at the breakfast room dining table grading exams. She is a tough math teacher and flunks students who do not meet her high standards; it's her duty to be strict, even though she anguishes with guilt at having to do it.

"All right, then. Sit down next to me." She opens the sealed envelope, looks at the grades and is silent.

"Did you see, Mom? Did you *SEE? **I got straight A's!**"*

My mother has a far-away look. Her head and spine are slightly curved down and immobile as if shouldering a very heavy weight. Then tears well up in her eyes and slowly trickle down her cheeks.

"Michael…oh, Michael." She shakes her head. Finally, she says softly, "Michael, all I ever wanted was a *normal* child."

She goes into her desk drawer and brings me her journal entry from long ago, when she was pregnant with me…

With me, as with the innumerable ones that have been and will be, first came God, then his plaything, a man, then that man's geometric progressions of offspring. I do not know the ones in between, but I know first there were Adam and Eve and shortly before my time there were some described in my beloved grandmother's handwriting in the following paper.

I was born, a cherished offspring to fulfill a great destiny. So my parents thought, and so thought I, as I grew feeling the sperm of greatness like a sore in my heart and abdomen. Some incredible luck and outer force seemed to drive me on to conquer, easily, without obvious effort, but with tremendous emotional stress and strain, the difficult and almost impossible.

I did not know it then, but the egg of greatness disintegrated when my first son was born. I've tried since, but after four years I realize that the spark, the drive, is gone, and I am so very glad. There is no more emotional tension from within, I relax and live each day without the charge of accomplishing any more than that, which is basic for my family and myself. The habit of tension is yet with me, but weakens every year that passes and I become more and more content and serene.

My children will not inherit the spark and drive I possessed and they will never do the extraordinary and I do not care at all. If they should be extraordinary, I would be glad, but they must never do the extraordinary out of inner compulsion, for it takes too much of a human being. They must live a natural, comfortable existence all their lives, as I shall, if God be willing.

— *Estelle Holloway King, 1954*

This difficult to compose medley describes the internal divisions within the black family structure and community due to the ongoing effects of a history of slavery.

CASTE WARS

For over a hundred years after Emancipation, the house slave and mixed-race minority carried both status and financial advantages. But such privileges came with a very steep price tag. Survival for house slaves demanded flawless obedience to convention and authority. They were forced to "read their master's mind" and meet his unspoken wants and expectations. House slaves were mere extensions of the master and his family, who saw them as objects to be exploited for personal gratification. And incestuous, or near incestuous, boundary violations became normal.

The racial mixing led to more and more Caucasian genetics and genetic defects that ultimately doomed the house slave caste to extinction, not unlike the pharaohs of ancient Egypt. The interbreeding was by choice, by rape, or by arranged marriages to one's own fair-skinned half-siblings and close cousins on the same or neighboring plantations. The mulatto caste would continue to almost exclusively interbreed for another century after Emancipation.

This type of abuse is less recognized, more nefarious, and rising in overall prevalence in America today. In such a case, the child becomes the "slave" of his or her parents—existing only to both gratify the parents' or owners' desires (sometimes, including sexually) *and* to swear mandatory secrecy—keeping the "family's sordid history." The child is dramatically wounded and is doomed to narcissistic predation for the rest of his or her life.

*

House slaves were afflicted by *psychological* torture, involving suppression of one's individuality and engulfment of one's boundaries. The house slave pattern of behavioral control was quite different from the *physical* aggression used to condition the field slaves. Like the transmission of brutal physical torture among the descendants of field slaves in childrearing practices, a devastating psychic wounding would be replicated for many generations post-slavery among the mixed-race house slave children. I sustained the house slave type of childhood conditioning from both my mother and father, whereas my darker-complexioned brother was more affected by physical abuse—such that the domestic child conditioning "matched" our respective pigmentations.

A caste system based on "shades-of-color" was created in slavery. The hierarchy elevated house slaves above field slaves, creating a division saturated loathing that still exists today. Originally, this was used to separate the two types of slaves from communicating household secrets or collaborating in a conspiracy against their masters, but later, the caste system severely affected their freed offspring. This hierarchy was carried onwards, wherein mixed-race descendants, the "high yellow" minority of African-Americans, inherited a shallow sense of self-worth based merely on one's degree of whiteness.

The field slaves deeply envied and resented the better status of the house slaves— their opportunity to live in the big house with material advantages of better food and clothing, and their subsequent economic opportunities due to having mixed genes with whites. The animosity harbored by the darker-complexioned towards the lighter-complexioned would persist as a caste war for the next one hundred and fifty years, and it *still* exists for many African descendants in both North and South America today.

*

BETRAYAL

The envy and hatred that my brother has had toward me since the beginning of my memory were so repressed that *only* at age fifty-eight, in therapy, did he realize that he'd *always* hated me. My brother does not see the transgenerational pattern of abuse.

At this point, Roy attributes his hatred simply to our father's "color bias"—my father's favoritism to me over my brother due to my lighter complexion and straighter hair. But the history of slavery reveals that there is more to the story. The shade-of-color caste structure elevated house slaves above the field slaves, creating a division saturated with fear and loathing that still exists today.

*

I am five years old. My mother tells my seven-year-old brother to take me outside the confines of the backyard and up to the corner of the block, perhaps ten houses away. He promises to take care of me and to not cross the intersection. I am so excited! I have never been beyond the yard without my mother before, and this seems like a grand adventure on a sunny summer afternoon.

Off we go, my brother first leading, then trailing behind me. We walk a few houses down the street to a driveway recess on the left, from which I hear a boy calling me, waving his hand.

"Come here!" he commands.

I look at my brother for guidance, but he says nothing. Since the other boy is older, about ten years old, I obey. He is white, probably Polish or Russian since this is a mixed colored and eastern European

54

area of town. He seems enormous to me and has a stern and sinister expression on his face.

I am now deep inside his driveway. My brother seems far away, lingering behind on the sidewalk of the street. The older kid tells me to stand with my back against the brick wall of his house. Then he gently, but insistently, pushes me to the wall. I am wedged into a narrow space; the brick wall at my back, the boy a few feet in front, and a red truck parked in the narrow alley driveway behind the boy.

I begin to panic. This was not supposed to be part of my walk to the corner. I can sense the boy's intentions and I see what's coming. The boy reaches into the open bay of the truck and lifts out a wooden baseball bat.

"Don't say anything and don't move!" he orders.

A snapshot is etched in my mind for years to come: My back is hugging the brick wall; the white boy with the wooden bat is three feet in front of me and a truck is just behind him. The only escape would be the narrow path from which I'd come, back to my brother. Why doesn't my brother help me?

I look at my brother in desperation, but he just stands where he is, grinning in frozen silence and intense curiosity. Like myself, my brother is also about to be engaged in a flash of neural restructuring: To *witness abuse* in such moments is to *learn to abuse* by deeply embedded example.

I cannot move now. My weak limbs are paralyzed. I cannot utter more than a barely audible high-pitched squeak as I watch, in slow motion, the assailant lift the bat high up over his right shoulder and then swing it with all his might toward my head.

CRACK! The bat pounds the brick wall. It has just missed my head, or I dodged an inch, I can't remember…Just then, a woman's voice calls from the house's interior, "Come upstairs, Billy! Your lunch is getting cold!"

The batter is momentarily distracted, looking up toward the voice. I take advantage of the opportunity to break away, running to the sidewalk—running without stopping. I dash all the way back to my yard and up to my third-floor apartment, crying red-hot tears of dismay that seem to never stop. My sibling has betrayed me. A lifetime pattern is set into karmic motion. I tattle on him to my mother and my mother becomes hysterical and beats him.

*

FIREFLIES

Just as the unconscious hatred and murderous impulses of my mother toward her *father* were displaced onto my helpless older *brother*, he then transferred the hating, hostile energy onto his safe victim— *ME*. My brother has always been oppositional and insulting toward me. The absence of kindness and support is woven with aggression that began when he was six years old. He would demarcate his territory and destroy any of my toys that accidentally crossed the imaginary line in our shared bedroom.

"Let's play doctor." he coaxed.

Soon, he stabs my eardrum with scissors.

I am eight years old. I am falling asleep in the early summertime night on my bed. My brother is outdoors and he knocks on the window adjacent to the head of my bed, calling my name sweetly. I open the window, and now there is only the mesh of a screen between the two of us. Excited, Roy, Junior shows me a jar filled with fireflies— *glow bugs*—that he's collected.

The dozens of bugs look magical in the twilight! Beautiful streams of incandescent color emanate from their round bodies. My brother unscrews the lid of the jar, catches one, and squeezes it into the screen— *—squashing out its flashing guts.* I am appalled as I watch the bug's greenish-white neon flashing entrails ooze down in front of my face.

Upon seeing my panicked reaction, my brother proceeds enthusiastically to squash more and more bugs through the screen. He is laughing at me as I watch the entire window screen become coated with incandescent slime.

Speechless, breathless, frozen and unaware of time, I cannot hear my mother calling me to the bathroom to bathe me. I don't know why she still feels obligated to bathe me at age eight. Finally, she yanks me out of my catatonic state.

I tell her what happened but she does not believe me, and she will not go to look at the window screen. "Your brother would *never* do a thing like that!" To this day, I have a phobia about harmless, little, plump bugs and gushy, colorful spiders.

*

SIBLING SABOTAGE

Roy, Junior, always found ways to terrify me and even to put my life at risk. Bruce and Roy became co-conspirators against me after the tent incident. An innocent winter game of "snowball fight" would become nearly lethal. My fluffy, soft snowballs were enough of a provocation for Roy and Bruce's escalated retaliation. I would be reduced to tears after being pelleted with densely packed, wet snow-and-ice balls, and jabbed with three-foot-long icicle spears, in volleys that felt like being stoned and stabbed to death.

Later, playing any board game with my brother was an incentive for him to bribe and make deals with any other players to entice them to gang up on me. Monopoly, Risk, Clue, Broadside, Dogfight, and Battleship were all hopeless ventures for me. Roy would take breaks to calculate the statistics of his moves and virtually guarantee winning. I never stood a chance. I was trounced as my brother smirked and scoffed at my stupidity. The only opportunity I had to avenge constant defeat was the *only* physically brutal game: "Rock'em Sock'em Robots." It's where Roy showed his truest nature and I dared manifest my retaliatory rage. "I'll knock your head off!" we both yelled.

It became clear that Roy, Junior was obsessed with scheming ways to hurt and humiliate me for the duration of my entire life. Both inside and outside the home, Roy would spread malicious gossip and fabricate derogatory lies about me, sometimes to my parents or partners, sometimes to his friends, sometimes to my peers, sometimes to my authority figures, sometimes to just anyone to whom he could talk.

The envy and hatred that my brother has had toward me since the beginning of my memory were so repressed that *only* at age fifty-eight, in therapy, did he realize that he'd *always* hated me. My brother does not see the transgenerational pattern of abuse.

At this point, Roy attributes his hatred simply to our father's "color bias"—my father's favoritism to me over my brother due to my lighter complexion and straighter hair. But the history of slavery reveals that there is more to the story. The shade-of-color caste structure created a division saturated with fear and loathing that still exists today.

*

FATHER'S DAY

My family is having dinner in a nice, new restaurant. I am seated with my mother to my right, my brother facing me sitting next to his daughter, and my father to my far right at the head of the table. It should be as it always is—predictable. It isn't. My mother opens and talks freely about her childhood memories, as my brother and I listen attentively to her stories.

"How was it growing up without any playmates, without any peers?" I ask.

"Well, at least, after age seven, I had my three cousins and when I was in high school, we went everywhere together," she replies with a faint smile.

"Who forced you to study and learn so assiduously, so precociously?" Roy asks.

"I was jealous of Narda, one of my cousins, who was four and a half and could read the newspaper. So, I asked my mother to teach me how to read at age four… and it all just flowed from there."

Somehow, the conversation leads to my mentioning the awards that I'd received in prep school. I ask my father if he remembers the awards, and that I was at the top of the class at Exeter. He admits that he'd never known anything about my achievements.

His ignorance was expected. I list my awards.

The fact that he listens to me and shows emotions, such as surprise, was a "first." But then he cuts me off; he proceeds to pull the topic over to how great a student *he* was, as the valedictorian at a small rural school. Dad insists on reciting his valedictorian speech lines from seventy years ago.

My brother engages me and gives me a card. "Why, Roy? *I'm* not a father." Rarely has a preprinted card meant something to me, but this one touches my heart:

There's a closeness that we share.
We don't discuss it, but it's there.
There's a corner of your heart reserved for someone special—
The person you're so proud to call your brother.

Roy then explains some of his revelations from doing trauma therapy, just as I am. "I've always hated you, Michael. I hated you because you were whiter looking, you could pass, and you were therefore Dad's favorite. I never stopped hating you until now." My brother's gaze and his words are matter-of-fact and directed not toward me, but to my parents who appear to not hear them at all.

This is the first time in my life that my brother has verbalized the unspoken truth. Roy has never shared anything about his personal life or feelings with me before.

And, it is true.

Roy and I recalled my father's trenchant color bias, the usual compliments about my being fair-skinned and having "good hair," while my brother was often teased with the cruel line, "Perhaps they made a mistake in the nursery." We both remembered how Dad's denigration was a daily occurrence, usually when Mom wasn't around to hear it. And how often Dad joked about "dark-skinned, stupid patients" over the dinner table, making faces when he'd answer a call from one.

Roy speaks louder to my parents and exclaims, "I'm *darker* than the two of you combined!"

My parents immediately object to the accusation of having any color bias, and my mother argues that my father *never* had any racial prejudice whatsoever. My brother and I both shake our heads in *simpatico*, in shared shame—burnt inside and lit to a visible flame from parental denial: "gas-lighting." What's the point of trying to lift their veil? My brother and I are bonding in our consensual truth.

It doesn't matter that my brother is attributing his hatred to just one factor, or my being "the favorite" to mere skin color. It doesn't matter that my sibling is still rationalizing his narcissistic hatred and minimizing the extent of his cruelty toward me, which spanned more than a half-century, with malicious set-ups and vicious subterfuge. What matters is that he finally confessed and spoke the secret truth that I've sensed and feared my whole life, ever since I was in a blind alley and about to be battered, when I glimpsed my brother's grin of insight.

I decide to test my brother's sincerity with just one such memory. "Roy, do you remember when we were hiking in the Southwest, doing the four-mile loop around the Great Meteor Crater in New Mexico, ten years ago?"

"Yep."

"Do you remember that the ferocious wind blew dirt in my eyes, so I had to take out my contact lenses and I was virtually blind?"

"Yes...."

"Then, do you remember that you suddenly got excited and told me to come quickly and see something?"

"Oh, sure."

"You guided me directly over a rock. You made me step within inches over a coiled rattlesnake. Roy—" I ask with my voice choking and tears entering my eyes, "Do you realize that I could have *died?*"

He does not answer verbally, but for the first time in my life, he doesn't laugh, mock, or deflect the gravity of his cruelty. I think I see a trickle of a tear enter his eyes, which mirror the glistening of real teardrops in mine. It is the first time that my only sibling has seemed to show any nuance of vulnerability, or any emotion other than anger toward me. I have never seen or heard him cry since the childhood beatings, perhaps since he was twelve years old.

In his spoken and silent confessions, I begin to forgive my brother's lifelong, ceaseless acts of hatred…the duplicity and the fabrications, the starting of rumors and the casting of aspersions, the refusal to ever teach me or share his knowledge with me, the utter absence of logistical help, and his constant efforts to turn others against me—my parents, my friends, my roommates, his spouses, and his children.

My brother and I sit in silence sharing the deep sorrow of age-old wounds. As we leave the restaurant, I feel closer to my brother than I've ever felt in my life. We were both victims of domestic violence, although in distinctly different ways. He whispers to me, "I can't believe how narcissistic Dad was."

I agree.

We hug before separating and driving home.

Two days later, my brother retracts any trace of culpability, regret, or apology about the rattlesnake incident. He concocts a farfetched rationalization for making me walk over the viper that reverses the roles of victim and abuser.

"Well, Michael, I recall that you'd *made* me take some LSD and I was therefore not thinking," he argues. The truth is that two days before the incident, my brother *asked* to take LSD with me, the effect had completely worn off, and his pleasure at putting me in danger was apparent in his taunting and hilarity immediately after I'd stepped over the snake.

But his ridiculous denial doesn't matter to me; it's just Roy, Junior, as always. What *does* matter was that he had at least a moment of remorse in the restaurant.

The following collection of short narratives further shows my cultural isolation due to having been exposed only to a white culture, with consequent confusion about my racial identity and hostility from other African Americans.

I am African-American by cultural identity, although both my brother and I carry a *record-breaking* number of racial chromosomes, as revealed by a Stanford geneticist in a recent book. Of *twelve* possible racial genotypes, I have somehow inherited *eleven*. My genes are roughly 52% European, 38% African and 10% Asian by chromosomal analysis, just

as are my brother's. The difference in pigmentation, which is based on only four gene pairs, is that he inherited the "black" Asian variant, while I inherited the "white" Asian gene in one of the four pairs.

One literary agent gave me pearls of inspiration, like "Yoda" to "Luke Skywalker" in *Star Wars*. Many of his observations were unforgettable: "You are the NEW AMERICA. You are the 'guinea pig' of American life. You're the perfect blend of races and complex circumstances."

*

LOOKING WHITE

Being mixed-race and passing for almost white was a source of pride as Dad grew up. My brother is ignored because he is darker. Dad often says I have "good hair," in contrast to my brother's "bad, kinky hair" —in front of my brother.

Dad instructs me on how to "look good." I must press hard on my wet hair, stroking it flat after a shower. Overnight, I wear the traditional and uncomfortable "stocking cap" made from my mother's discarded nylons. In the morning, I carefully remove the cap and rush to the mirror to make sure no curls remain.

"You must look *GOOD*, Michael," he says.

Mom's infinite instructions were as strict as her maternal great-grandmother, who was head schoolmarm of a boarding school for Creole débutantes. She teaches me to "e-*nun*-ci-ate" perfectly, frequently correcting my diction. She makes me stand with my spine flat against a wall to learn "correct posture."

"You must look *PROUD*, Michael," she says.

I turn my full lips inwards, to make them appear thinner. Thus, they become painfully chapped from my saliva and I become dependent on ChapStick for relief. I push up the tip of my nose, squeeze the bridge, and pull down on the sides of my nostrils—just like my mother had done as a child. I pray that I can make it grow straight, narrow, and aquiline. But my nose doesn't change.

I must look *WHITE*, I think.

A photograph of myself at age six in 1960

*

WHAT THE HELL ARE YOU?

A new YMCA has just opened in Erie near my home in the suburbs. My single white friend and I decide to check it out. The anxiety about being the first non-white has become a normal and controllable fear, even though the idea of going to *any* YMCA evokes a sensation of drowning.

But I have a white protector and I've learned valuable survival skills. We check our belongings in at the bag counter and I receive a token to wear around my wrist while I explore the pool and the new Jacuzzi. When I've seen enough of the facility, I decide to leave on my own, while my friend stays longer.

I approach the middle-aged lady at the bag check counter, present my token, and politely ask for my bag. "Hello, Ma'am. Could I have my gym bag, please?" She hesitates for an uncomfortable, seemingly interminable, length of minutes as she stares at me with intense concentration and bewilderment.

I ask again for my bag of belongings, but she refuses to get it—*not until I answer her pressing question:* "What the hell are 'ya? You ain't white, you ain't black...Are you **Injun?**" she blurts out.

A photograph of myself at age 15 as I start 10th grade at Exeter

*

YOU'RE PAKISTANI

The rumor spreads among the teachers that I am Martin Luther King's nephew. Only *famous* people belong at Exeter, so I let it slide. White classmates stay aloof: they know I'm just black and "ordinary." When the movie "A Separate Peace" is filmed at the school, a memo goes out that blacks must stay outside of the filming area "because it is not consistent with the 1950's era in which the film is based." I am used to racism and I have my ways to avenge it.

The shame of abandonment I'd felt for being "not white" in Erie takes on another dimension; I discover that I am also "not black." The anticipation of finally knowing other blacks erodes into this new and disappointing level of ostracization. After my first year at Exeter, I ask the president of the support group for the fifty non-white students, the "Afro-Exonian Society," why I'd not been invited to a single meeting. "Because you're *Pakistani*," he replies.

"You ain't *white*, you ain't *black*, you ain't *Injun*—are you...***A-rab***?"

*

YOU'RE ITALIAN

I see two black girls outside the gate peering toward the house with curiosity. I approach them graciously; I open the gate and step onto the sidewalk to introduce myself. "Hi. I'm Michael King. Would you two like to come join the party? It's open."

Both the girls look down at the sidewalk with their hands in their pockets. One slowly moves her foot back and forth and doesn't answer. The other replies quietly, "No, we can't. It's a *white* party."

The shuffling girl stares at me, then looks down again. She speaks slowly. "You're Michael King. I recognize you! I was in 7th grade at James S. Wilson Junior High School. You were in the 9th grade. They put me in the special classes, but I saw you in the halls."

"Wow! I thought that I was the *only* black student in the school! What a surprise! How come I never saw you?" I exclaim.

Her reply enters like a bullet. "*Nobody* ever saw me because I'm slow and I'm black. Besides, why would *you* have seen me? I was the only little black girl in the school and there was nobody else black but me. *You're Italian!*"

The teenage girls walk off slowly and silently, dragging their feet on the pavement, back into the ghetto. They soon disappear under a melancholy blanket of darkness and invisibility.

*

YOU'RE A BLACK CHEROKEE

Rehab will be a complete flashback to my childhood, nearly half a century earlier. Concord quickly rears its three monstrous heads of racism, homophobia, and working-class bigotry. I am about to be harassed, hazed, and physically assaulted for the next five weeks. I won't sleep a single night in rehab without dreading the next traumatic exposure to the multi-headed demonic dragon.

It's my second morning in the detox unit. I will finally have my medical intake by the ward physician, Dr. Van Reich. I enter the medical staffroom and sit facing a white doctor who scans me eerily. Then he asks what I do for a living.

"I'm a physician."

"Where did you go to school?"

"Harvard."

He leans back in his chair, momentarily crestfallen. Next, he begins to demonstrate his dominance to overcome his envy. He boasts that he has run the unit for thirty years and could detox anybody. His next question stuns me: "So, what *race* are you?"

"I'm mixed race. Caucasian and black…."

"What *else* are you?"

"Well, I'm part American Indian. That means Asian genes."

"Which *TRIBE*?"

"Cherokee, but also…"

He cuts me short with a shout of glee: "So you're a *BLACK CHEROKEE!* Of course, you're an alcoholic!"

For the next thirty minutes, he rants about his proud Nazi heritage, claiming his father was the field marshal who attempted to assassinate Hitler. He boasts about his money and property, his cars and boats. He asks me nothing about my problems. Narcissists are like that…

*

KEEP DANCING

The schism between Erie and Exeter deepens into a rift as wide as the Grand Canyon.

It's my first summer break from Exeter and I'm back in Erie. A dance at the Booker T. Washington Center is announced in the newspaper. I yearn to meet the black peers who I had never known and whose support I'd needed so much in the all-white schools. Fortunately, I have a driver's license now and I can sneak away without parental permission. 'Why had they always kept me apart from other blacks?' I wonder.

I feel nervous, but an ardent internal drive for acceptance prods me on. There is nobody to greet me at the door as I walk into a large room with a wood floor. I am thrilled to find about forty black youngsters my age mingling together. The music hasn't started yet; it's social chat time. I timidly walk over to a group of three girls and introduce myself.

"Hi. I'm Michael King and this is my first time here. Who are you?"

In response, I receive only stares. They resume chatting with each other and ignore me. I wonder if perhaps they don't feel comfortable with a stranger, but I'm *not* a stranger. Surely they know of my family! My father probably delivered them as babies.

"Hello! I'm Michael King! You know—Dr. King's son. I'm glad to meet you!" It gets their attention, but not in a good way.

"So, *you're* one of the *KING BOYS!*" an attractive girl with long black hair replies loud enough for others to hear. "Sure, we know about your family. Why you talk so funny? Where *you* go to school?"

Taken aback and without an easy answer, I want to change the subject. But my speech *is* so different from theirs. "Uh…I go to a school in New England now."

The girl fakes an attempt at a haughty English accent. "Well, well, well. Aren't you the *crème de la crème*! HEY! EVERYBODY! He goes to school in *England!* And you live in a nice big house, too. Can I be your maid?" She seems to hate me and I can't understand why.

The music starts and she asks me if I want to dance. I'm not a good dancer, but I would certainly try. Her movements are wild, pulsating, pelvic, and fast. It's some new popular dance style I don't know but I've seen on "American Bandstand." I can't follow her and she seems to *want* to make me look like a bad dancer.

Then, she abruptly stops dancing with me and joins the others, directing them to look at me. My near vision suddenly blurs and I feel a strange energy on my skin. I'm standing alone on the dance floor. I know, *before* I look around, that I am being looked at by unfriendly energy.

The other forty youths have formed a tight circle around me; they are pointing and gawking at me, hissing and mocking…

Derision replete with stinging words: "He the *rich* King boy! He go to prep'tory school in England. Look at him dance and talk like a *white boy* and think he's *better* than us!"

My brown skin is burning as if tied to a stake with flames crisping all the way up to my hair. I stop dancing and just stand still but the room is spinning around me. Swirling, swarming fingers *pointing*, mouths distorted with *revulsion*, ghetto jargon that I don't understand…

The hostile energy is closing in on me.

The girl has instigated a mob atmosphere and shouts out, "Keep dancing! Will ya' look at *that!* You should see 'ya self! *A spec-ta-cle!* KEEP DANCING! BOURGEOIS OREO!"

"KEEP SWIMMING!"
"I dash and run for my life through the familiar woods."
"I HATE YOU!"

THE ARYTHMIC DRUMBEAT IS A RAPID LIGHT DIZZY ACHE IN MY HEAD

I'm choking in shame as I push my way through the circle and run off before the "spectacle" escalates even more. I've failed another test.

When I get home, I tell my mother what had happened. She offers no solace, only aggravated criticism. "Well, of course! Why on Earth would you want to mingle with *that* class of people? I've *tried* to protect you, Michael. You should have listened to me. You should have known better!"

*

I'M WHITER THAN YOU

I've just turned seventeen and it's my freshman year at Harvard College. My roommate was placed in the same room with me simply because he was an Exeter graduate and he's black. I've never met him before. He's a charity case student who was lucky to get into the program "Upward Bound," designed to rescue the poorest, yet intelligent, blacks from the Deep South and urban ghettoes.

His grades are mostly C's and he pronounces "Don Quixote" as "Don Quick-Zot." He puts straightening grease in his hair that makes the doorknob slippery and hard to open. It has a strong smell, as does his single pair of shoes.

"You're no better than me!" he says disdainfully. "You got better hair, but I'm a whiter color than you." It's true; he has a sallow, "pale milky" color and I have a swarthy, "slightly-soiled" color. He grew up in the South, fatherless, picking cotton along with ten siblings and often going hungry. We argue about "Who had it worse" in life. I can't even get him to *imagine* all that I'd suffered. He envies me because I grew up with money and I have access to money now. It's the field slave hostility toward the house slave, all over again.

*

BLACK VERSUS BROWN

Christmas recess from college is coming up. My brother and I decide that we want a real adventure, on our own and without parental supervision. Haiti has been off-limits for Americans for ten years, under the dictatorship of "Papa Doc" Duvalier. Papa Doc died a few months ago, the travel prohibition has just been lifted, and the people are rejoicing. Why not go join them?

My nineteen-year-old brother has a grant from Cornell to study Haitian voodoo art, and I am finally successful arguing my case with my parents to be allowed to accompany him. Perhaps, American history at Exeter has paid off; I can debate fiercely now.

With the stipulation that we'd have a chaperone, we could go to Haiti for three or four weeks. My mother contacts an old friend from her graduate school days who lives in Port-au-Prince; she agrees to "take good care of us." With my mother feeling some relief, I am free to go with the belief that my mother's former classmate will closely monitor me.

Roy has a secret agenda that he shares with me, "Let's find out about voodoo. Could be fun, eh?" In my mind, I see him spinning the globe of the world and I nonchalantly agree to check it out, but I don't believe in superstitious things like that. Even if there's some danger, I speak French fluently, I'm sort of black, I'm innocently young, and I'm American—all factors that should protect me from harm. Besides, we'll have a three-room suite in a swanky, well-guarded hotel, with meals cooked on the grounds under sanitary conditions.

I arrive in Port-au-Prince and the mood is *not* celebratory. I wasn't prepared for such poverty. Outside of the airport, there are over-crowded streets where the poor must dash across, because those in vehicles honk their horns and don't slow down for the pedestrians. I see blocks of smoky Shantytown huts. There are lines of emaciated women, some pregnant and some with withered old faces, trudging barefoot through muddy roads with heavy urns of water and staples balanced on their heads.

I wasn't prepared for such wealth. There are concrete mansions as large as a city block. Barbed-wire walls and electronic gates, and several guards with guard dogs, surround the estates. I meet the wealthy family that is chaperoning us. They live in a gated villa near the hotel and have a daughter who's sixteen, named "Sibyl." She has long reddish hair and a cute oval-shaped face. I've already begun to flirt with her. The family is like myself—light-complexioned racial hybrids.

I meet a friendly young man who's attending college in the Dominican Republic. He strolls with me on the road *en route* to see Sibyl. When we arrive at the gate, I invite him to come inside with us.

He looks down, shaking his head. The watchman at the gate is staring at him and tells us to please wait a moment.

"Both the girls look down at the sidewalk with their hands in their pockets. One slowly moves her foot back and forth and doesn't answer."

The guard comes back with Sibyl who whispers to me in French, "That man is not the right kind of people you should be with." My new friend whispers in my other ear, "They won't let me in. I'm too dark-skinned. It's a light-skinned house."

Sibyl takes my brother and me to her private club where I order a rum and coke. The customers are all mulatto and the waiters are all dark-complexioned. I ask Sibyl why there is such tension in Haiti. "Papa Doc" is dead and things should be all rosy now.

"Shhh! We can't talk about *politics*." She whispers, frightened. "Any one of the waiters could be a spy. If there's a dark one around, *be quiet!*"

She introduces me to a customer at another table near the pool. He's the Haitian ambassador to France and I'm honored to meet him. Later that afternoon, the ambassador picks me up at the hotel in a Mercedes-Benz and drives me to his villa on the coast. I watch with astonishment as one of his workers climbs like an acrobat up to the top of a tall coconut tree, cuts a coconut loose, and tosses it down to another worker—all in a few seconds.

The Ambassador explains the political situation in his private study while I sip the fresh coconut milk through a straw. "When the French left, they gave all the land to their mixed-race offspring. The mulattos then created an institution of *neo*slavery over the others and skin color was associated with money, education, *everything*. I'm from the mulatto caste. We funded the military that kept us secure for a very long time and it was a decent way for the poor, the darker ones, to make money."

I notice the Ambassador's face suddenly has a faraway look. His eyelids stay wide open without blinking for several minutes. He shakes his head to bring himself back into the room and continues.

"Then, in 1957, Papa Doc got the support of the army and instigated a partial revolution against us, *a slave insurrection,* so to speak. Papa Doc was an expert in voodoo and he ruled with brutal terror. He had a ruthless security force, known as the 'Tontons Macoutes.' They were real-life bogeymen, real zombies, who routinely executed Papa Doc's opponents. That's when the Americans blockaded the island. Now, the dark people have military power, but we still have the money and land."

He adds quietly, "It's a war between black and brown."

This is one of my favorite pieces, depicting extreme racism within the elitist world of the prestigious Phillips Exeter Academy.

HATE MOTIVATES

My defense strategy of intellectualization suddenly tapped into my earlier years of pent-up rage and muffled defiance, even hatred. I commenced to repress my tender sentiments and vulnerable feelings under a heavy mantel of intellectual arrogance. I began to use my intellect as an *offensive* maneuver to decimate others and vindicate or glorify myself. That's what everybody seemed to do at Exeter, so it was condoned and even encouraged.

I had to sharpen my intellect, because, eventually…I knew there would come a time when I would have to stand up for myself and risk everything to preserve my brittle little nugget of self-esteem at the Academy.

I've been selected for the top division in the ultimate course at Exeter: American history. It's a direct link to a political career and my teacher, my "Master," is the venerable Dr. Schultz, who, I am told, used to teach at Harvard Law School. Rumors surround him: He is reputably the *toughest* teacher of the *toughest* course at the *toughest* school in America.

I'm prepared for class today; I've crammed everything possible about the historical period of 1820-1845. But I've also learned that what happens in class has little to do with preparation or with American history.

I'm sitting around the lustrous Harkness table with seven other nervous students. We all scramble for a seat as far away from Dr. Schultz as possible. I arrived at class early today, running from my previous class, and lucked out. I get the precious "most-distant" chair.

Dr. Schultz starts to tell us the rules of the term paper. Primary, secondary, and tertiary research required; long hours reading old manuscripts, newspapers, affidavits, and collecting data from microfiches archived in the library are expected. Perfect notations and references in the bibliography are mandatory.

Then, he pauses and organizes some papers. 'What *now?* Another exam?' I wonder. I anticipate the unanticipated in this class. 'Or will it be *my* turn for attack today?'

"Uh, hum. *MISTER KING*," Dr. Schultz vociferates.

"Yes, professor?" My startled voice screeches. The other students exhale with relief; they're off the radar and off the hook for today.

"WE WILL DEBATE! The subject is slavery. I will take the side of *pro-slavery* and you will be the *abolitionist.* We will debate the issue consistent with the facts of the historical period." For him, this is a familiar game. To debate means to practice for the defense; he always takes the position of the prosecutor.

"The institution of slavery is indubitably a benevolent system to protect the financial stability of civilization. Furthermore, slavery has limitless historical precedent. The only question is: *Whom* to enslave?" Schultz speaks with a flippant, yet terse, tone. I begin my defense on moral grounds and Constitutional equality.

"The Constitution declares as equal only those who are *fully* human. The Negro is incapable of such standards. His is a sub-human savage as evidenced by his bestial lack of culture and deficient self-restraint in the jungles of Africa. Slavery uplifts him to the useful function of supervised labor. Even more, the institution of slavery protects him from *himself.* It keeps him from reverting back to savagery," Schultz declares.

I point out that sophisticated cultures existed in Africa that surpassed tribal law and...

"MISTER KING! There are *no* anthropological or sociological studies of such nature *whatsoever* at this historical time in America. Those fields did not even exist! Stick to the evidence and argument of the time!"

I am sweating. I must not let him detect my trembling. His laser-sharp stare burns through bifocals that magnify his eyes and pierce my brain.

I *wrack* my brain: What can I pull from my crammed memory about this topic? It was not on the reading list. I've *got* to find an impenetrable defense. Why is he picking on *me?* I'm the only black student in the class. I'm probably the *only* black student he's ever had! DAMN IT!" I flash back on the story of "Daniel Webster and the Devil."

He resumes, "The Negro brain is one-half the size of the white brain."

"But that's not *true!*" I protest, choking.

"Stick to the argument of the time!" He reprimands again, and then continues with an irate and impatient tone. "Dissections of Negro brains are scientific proof that the Negro brain is grossly inferior to the white brain."

I blank out. Debate? A rapid exchange of verbal quips and argument alternating with *counter*-argument fill a space of dilated time. I have left my body and I am a slave arguing for my *own* freedom. I've *got* to prove that I have a right to get free. I feel my wracked body and cauterized skin. I am *bound* to a whipping *stake*. I am bound to get free! My life is at stake! I SNAP.

I abruptly shove my chair back and stand up. I grab my papers and books and clutch them over my sunken chest. I will break the cardinal rule and walk out of this cage! The door slams as I leave the classroom.

'Not allowed to ever leave the classroom without explicit permission under any circumstances—or an immediate probation order will be issued.'

I step onto the marble floor of a vast domed hallway. I cannot walk any farther for my legs are now completely frozen and weak. I lean against a twenty-foot-high wall covered with gold-framed portraits of illustrious principals and benefactors, dating back over two hundred years. My knees give way and I slowly slide down the wall and sink to the floor next to a pedestal with the bust of a prestigious head on top.

Hot, hateful, humiliated tears stream down my cheeks. What will become of me now? Dr. Schultz is known to be sadistic. A petrified voice in my head whispers, 'I've run away and I will be caught and punished.' Time warps to the infinite moment of the speed of light. There are voices speaking inside the classroom, yet I can also "hear" the snowflakes falling outside the huge arched cathedral window to my far right.

I hate Schultz! I vow I'll get a goddamn **A** in the American history course. I will *win* the most coveted prize in this *fucking* academy! I'll show him! I'll get that history prize! Then, I'll get out of this school! *MY* brain is not inferior!

The classroom door opens and slams again. Without looking, I psychically know he's not Dr. Schultz. A benevolent energy kneels beside me and places his arm on my shoulder. I look up. Through the fog of the wet blurry snowflakes of my tears, I make out the face of one of my classmates who has dared to defy the rules and become a co-conspirator with me.

A Shining Knight of Camelot kneels beside me and comforts me with his words, "That was *wrong* what he did to you, Michael. I will stand beside you on this. And I know my family will, too!" This time, the messenger is Robert Shriver, nephew of the late President

Kennedy. The message comforts me deep inside, "You can be yourself and that's OK, Michael."

And, I *won* the most-coveted American history prize. I also won the academy's French and religion prizes, more prizes than any other student. I'm sixteen and ready to skip my senior year to enter Harvard College.

This very short memoir takes place my second year at Harvard College, age eighteen. It simplistically captures the oppressive nature of an elitist education and my late adolescent rebellion against social stratification that excludes me— merely because of race and privilege.

SOCIOLOGY 101

I've decided to take Sociology 101. I'm excited to take an introduction to sociology; it should be interesting and complement my studies in psychology and cross-cultural issues. Sociology: the field of social behavior and fascinating differences between world cultures, family units, and leadership. Wow!

The lecture hall amphitheater is packed with about two hundred Harvard classmates. The excited hubbub abruptly ceases when an august gentleman in a three-piece suit and bowtie enters and approaches the podium. He is the chairman of the department of sociology, Dr. George C. Homans, the Third.

He speaks into the microphone, "Good morning." A hush ripples through the room. I look around and see that I am the only non-white student. 'With my impressive Afro and hand-made dashiki shirt, I am clearly the odd-ball here,' I think.

The professor begins his lecture. "As you all know, in our culture there is an upper-class, a middle-class, and a lower-class." His commanding voice scales with the words: high-pitched, middle-pitched, and low-pitched tones.

"But how *many* of you know that there is an UPPER-upper-class, a MIDDLE-upper-class, a LOWER-upper-class, an UPPER-middle-class, a MIDDLE-middle-class...."

As his pompous voice drones from a very high pitch and drops down a few notes with each stratification, I feel myself slipping away and leaning harder against the back of my seat. His words pass right through my head like a sound wave echoing out to the beyond.

"And for those of you who would *like* to know, *I* am a member of the *UPPER*-upper-class! By the criteria of aristocratic genealogy, dating back to the ruling Stuarts of England, and by race, property, education, culture, habits, breeding…."

I am feeling the sword of rage erupt in my seventeen-year-old loins and rise as a gushing tsunami into my head. I glare at George C. Homans, *the Third*, with unmistakable hatred. After class, a cluster of eager students gathers around him at the lectern and I elbow my way through them. He backs off upon my approach, cautiously.

I spew without premeditation, "Your ancestors were rum-drinking, slave-trading, witch-burning, incestuously inbred hypocrites, *MISTER* Homans!" Then I turn and walk away, leaving the professor dumbfounded.

Class after class, I glare at Professor Homans with the intention of learning nothing from him *whatsoever*. I change the course to pass-fail, which I'll easily swing, but I don't drop it. I must make him squirm as I sit boldly near the front row, but on the far side of the amphitheater so I can escape if necessary.

He continues his inane lectures on the social strata of 13th century English villagers, about which I don't give a damn. From time to time, he pauses and returns my glare. I can play that game, too—*a stare-down!* Then, one day he stops the lecture and we lock eyes for quite a while.

Finally, he says, "I don't know what *some* of you are thinking about *me* right now." He pauses. "But I shall tell you this: What *I* think of *you* does not matter." Another pause. For drama, I wonder? "*And what you THINK I THINK of you matters even less!*"

This course has value, after all. I finally get it. I relax.

In this shocking journalistic piece, I recount witnessing the ongoing savage enslavement of blacks in the remote jungles of Colombia.

THE KILLING FIELDS

I'd always fantasized that I could use my love of languages and psychology by traveling to places where my ethnic identity didn't matter. So, I specialized in international public health. Regrettably, I discovered that my healing qualities were *not* wanted abroad. The Good Ship Hope of the liberal Sixties was sinking for the Third World.

My usefulness in the Third World would be limited to gathering epidemiological data and compiling statistics. I don't enjoy that; I enjoy helping human beings. I also discovered how unpopular it is to be known as an American abroad.

"So, you work for the CIA?" strangers would suddenly ask me. In addition, the risk of being kidnapped was always very high for Americans. But I was lucky; speaking the native languages fluently and having my skin color allowed me to pass unidentified as an American in most places near the equator.

When I took up international studies at Johns Hopkins, my faculty advisor quietly added the *final* caution: "In half of the Third World countries where you'll be sent, especially in Nigeria where you'll be for the upcoming two years, the penalty for homosexuality is *death.*"

Still, I went to work and live abroad as a volunteer on student loans. Although the experiment to work as a "healer" failed, I learned some vital life lessons. And what I discovered changed my life forever...

*

Apartadó, Colombia
1979

I'm filled with anxious anticipation: My medical school has arranged for me to work in a jungle hospital in South America doing tropical medicine. I've spent a few weeks going around to teaching hospitals in Boston to get boxes of syringes, gloves, surgical equipment, intravenous supplies—whatever is about to be discarded or not needed in America. The jungle hospital doctors look forward to such gifts. About once a year or so, the same remote hospital will greet a student from Harvard and show him or her what it's like "down there."

I've read about Apartadó. The place has captivated the imagination, concerned the conscience, and catalyzed the restless subconscious of great novelists like Gabriel Garcia Marquez in his Nobel-prize winning book, "One Hundred Years of Solitude." I've studied the novel; it describes the massacre of thousands of banana workers in 1929, slaughtered by agents of wealthy plantation owners. The workers had protested slave-like working conditions.

The *restless* subconscious, the *troubled* subconscious, and the *terrified* subconscious...

In the end, *only* my subconscious will be able to put the pieces together.

I'm aboard a small airplane flying from Medellín to Apartadó, where I will spend the next three or more months. The security check of my boxes of medical supplies is unexpectedly detailed before departure. I look around the twenty-seat plane; I see one casually dressed man in the rear and I see eighteen uniformed military men with lots of brassy medals. The energy in the plane is tense and quiet.

I don't yet know what's been happening in Apartadó over the past half year. I don't realize that Apartadó is still living in 1929, only worse. I am not prepared for seven decades of terror.

When we land in Apartadó, a squadron of saluting soldiers is in formation as the officers walk off the plane. My baggage and medical supplies are checked again and again. I try to explain that they are going to the city hospital, but only by grace of the intervention of an officer—
—a colonel, I think—can my boxes be allowed to pass into the sultry blazing jungle world of tropical enchantment.

A taxi takes me to the regional hospital. The mood is as heavy as the humid sweat of my clothes. The hospital's medical director and seven young male doctors, who are fulfilling their required year's work in an underserved area before licensure, all greet me without smiles.

Seven? I'd been told there were eight rural resident doctors. The medical director takes me aside. Yes, there *were* eight until last week when a physician was "disappeared." I question my understanding; perhaps my Spanish translation is wrong. "The doctor treated a guerilla fighter for battle wounds. He did not report the guerilla to the paramilitary militias. The paramilitaries found out," the director quietly explains. Then, he reiterates, louder, "The doctor was taken away. *He was disappeared.*"

Years later, I'll watch the movie "Chicken Run" and witness the scene where the rebel chicken is caught escaping, then thrown into the coal bin as punishment. I'll hear the chicken farmer's words and flash back to Apartadó: "And let that be a lesson for the whole *lot* of you!"

The Medical Director adds, "Curfew is at 6pm—set your watch. You *must* be inside the hospital walls before 6pm." Suddenly, I'm getting a queasy feeling about Apartadó.

The next morning, I stroll into the town on my own; it's about a mile and a half from the hospital. Apartadó is a quaint town of only eighty thousand people and little more than one bustling main street where the open-air marketplace is set up.

I meet a skinny and unhealthy looking local fellow who wants to befriend me and invites me to his cottage. He is probably gay and he's a "stoner." He asks me if I want to try some local hashish, and soon sells me a huge ball of opium-grade hashish for five dollars that will last an entire year.

Time goes by as we chat, stoned, sitting on his back porch. I ask him what it's like to live in Apartadó. Before he can answer, he points to a fruit tree in his yard and a solid two-foot wide black streak coming out of the jungle and climbing up the tree. I've never seen army ants before. My new friend is furious and grabs a bucket of poison powder. He leads me to the swath of ants that are invading his tree. I look closely and I learn...

The ants are big, menacing, red, and armed with pincer-sharp mandibles. They march in nearly perfect military precision toward their target. My acquaintance dumps some poison onto the middle of the infinite brigade. Chaos breaks out; the dying ants stray from the linear formation and spread out around the poison. When a rivulet of sick ants deviates, thousands of other ants pounce on and attack the sick ones—chopping them up into pieces. Instantly, the poisoned bedlam turns into a frenzied murderous mass *free-for-all* of *all-against-all*.

"*That* is Apartadó!" My new friend exclaims. Meanwhile, his fruit tree has been completely defoliated and consumed. Sometimes, one's subconscious intuition speaks louder than the facts. What was actually happening in Apartadó was sheer madness. It was too complex to ever piece together by logic.

I look at my watch—it is 6:10 pm. I panic! I've *got* to get back to the hospital. I run as fast as I can along the roadway, mostly in the deep muddy ditches on its sides for cover, scanning ahead and behind, then looking at my watch in disbelief. Whenever I see a military vehicle approaching, I huddle in the drainage trench, and then I dash off again.

I lie, panting, sweating, back in my private room. I look up at the ceiling fan above my bed as it wobbles from a loose mounting, wondering how it will chop *my* body up into pieces when it breaks loose and falls on me in my sleep.

"My nightmares started after seeing the movie, "The Pit and the Pendulum," and the ultimate sacrificial platform upon which the victim was bound and watching a huge blade ratcheting down to slice open his belly."

The next morning, I go to inspect the slaughterhouse and ask how they test the cows for disease. The toothless butcher points to the group of cows huddled together, waiting. Then he points to a single cow, separate from the herd. "If the cows avoid *that* one, it's probably diseased. That's our only test." Inside the slaughterhouse I watch as a cow's throat is slit with a machete and it exsanguinates. I avert my eyes when its front legs collapse.

I go to the open market where the meat and fish are covered with swarms of flies. It smells of rotten garbage. I test the milk, but only for specific gravity to see how much it has been diluted with water. Sometimes, I write a "warning" to the vendors. They just shrug their shoulders and don't seem to care.

I take a very long hike up into the mountainous jungle with one of the doctors, climbing to the *toma de agua*, which is the water supply for the town. It's far upstream from major contamination, but still an amoebic soup. I come back sunburned, walking past miles of banana trees with plastic bags over the pale green clusters of bananas that are ready for export. I see one that's ripe and walk over to pluck and eat it.

"Don't take it!" The other doctor yells. "*Nobody* can have it. Not even if you're starving. It's for export to America only. If they see you, you'll be beaten or killed."

HUSH! There are times and places when the "hide and play dead response" is completely natural and warranted for survival against human predation. The town and the hospital are muffled under a blanket of sultry shame and a tense deathly silence. Only by bits and pieces—the expressions on people's faces, whispered conversations and strange events—do I eventually begin to understand.

Most Apartadó residents are poor black or mulatto workers, who are descendants of escaped slaves—the *cimarrones* of centuries past. After only a century of freedom, they were eventually reclaimed by whites and *re*-enslaved. Since it was after the official abolition of formal slavery, it's called *neoslavery*.

The countless courageous men of African ancestry are loaded onto trucks from neighboring, partitioned off, all-black coastal provinces. They will live in crowded shanties on the plantations and receive subsistence wages. They must work from dawn to dusk in forced separation from their families.

I have never seen real slavery. Many of these workers are my patients, and they bear the wounds and scars of brutality. The morgue is already full of those who have protested their conditions, who have tried to unionize or to escape back to freedom.

Sometimes, a worker hires a prostitute in the town. Sometimes, he vents his rage on the prostitute, especially when she is busy with another client. That means a lot of tendon repair practice on women's wrists, slashed by machetes.

The workers and the poor town folk support the guerrillas of the Revolutionary Armed Forces of Colombia (FARC) because the left-wing guerrillas support the workers' efforts to unionize. The sympathetic town residents supply provisions for the guerrillas.

Just before I'd arrived, FARC splintered into three internal warring factions over minor ideological differences. Each faction now attacks the other two; each claim separate jungle regions and has secured the loyalty of their "barrios," or slum communities. The ultimate madness: Left-wing guerrillas with minor political differences are *united* against the paramilitary groups and against the Colombian army, and simultaneously *divided* and killing themselves.

The plantation owners are right-wing fanatics who exploit the black work force and suppress all attempts for the workers to unionize or seek better conditions. They sell their bananas to the Chiquita Banana Company or to Dole Fresh Food Company in the United States. Chiquita Banana, and possibly also Dole, supports the rich plantation owners, who exploit their workers, who then supply the guerrillas, who fight the military and the paramilitaries and each other. I am stuck in the middle of warring factions and murderous vendettas...

The chaos is American-made, just because Dole and Chiquita Banana want a good profit and don't care how they get it. The exportation-exploitation rule is like the Colombian exports of textiles, leather, coffee, and something else. A neoslavery slogan begins to repeat itself in my mind: *"American-made, but not made-in-America."*

Apartadó represents the historical paragon of oppression and the threat of violence is always very near. It's a town renowned for exportation and exploitation. And it is a *strategic* town, only forty miles away from Panama—thus it exports more than just bananas.

A plantation magnate invites me to see his *finca,* or ranch, as the guest of honor from America. What he *earnestly* wants me to see is his point of view and to transmit it to the American press. As we ride on horseback around his extensive plantation grounds and private columned estate, he tries to impress upon me that the guerillas are bad, they're *Communists*... They kidnap ranchers for ransom, and they've murdered...

My brother grins as he asks me,
"Well, what if they're good and we're bad? What if they're just like us?"

The wealthy plantation owner takes me into a barn to show me his pigs. One of his men follows us with a rifle. My host asks me which pig I like best. 'What a strange question!' I think. But I look for the sweetest and most cuddly looking pig I can find and point to it.

The rifleman instantly shoots it dead. I watch as men cut its gut open, remove its entrails, and set it ablaze to burn off its hair and toast its ears. Then, they hack off an earlobe and give it to me to eat; it's a delicacy that makes me nauseated.

Late that afternoon, I meet an old grandmother who is now "godmother." Her house has become an orphanage for babies the prostitutes don't want or whose parents have been murdered. She has thirteen orphaned children and most are at the age when they can learn to read. The grandmother has been illiterate her whole life, but now she is learning to read so that she can read to the children and teach them to read, too.

The first book that she is learning and reciting is not the Holy Bible. It's "The Communist Manifesto," by Karl Marx.

She struggles to recite: *"Religion is the sigh of the oppressed creature, the heart of a heartless world, just as it is the spirit of a spiritless situation. It is the opium of the people."*

Damn! It's after curfew again. I repeat the mad dash back to the hospital, evading lorries, and running in the roadside ditches. It's too dangerous to use a flashlight.

The metal gates of the hospital ER are opened at 8am to endless lines of the sick and dying who cram to get in. They have already been waiting for many hours and sometimes many days, but there's just too many to treat and most are sent away.

One morning, there *isn't* a line when I open the ER doors; instead, a black van is parked outside, waiting for just that moment. A naked man's body is tossed out from the back of the van, rolls on the dirt ground, and lands at my feet. He is bound at his wrists and ankles and has a gag in his mouth.

One of the doctors explains the scenario because he's used to it. The victim had been beaten, tortured, and then tied naked to a tree in the jungle for many days. The tree was in a swampy mosquito-plagued area where the deadly strain of *Falciparum* malaria is endemic. This is the worst type of malaria possible—it makes the blood clot in your brain. When the paramilitaries were certain that he'd been infected and his brain was "erased," they gave him to the hospital as a patient. He didn't survive.

I opt out and try to be invisible. I have never wanted to be *more* invisible than during those three long months. I put together the hospital's first general anesthesia machine; up until now, surgeries, amputations, and invasive tests were all done fully awake. The assembly instructions are in English, so I'm selected to set it up. Then, I get to test the nitrous oxide on myself.

The big ball of hashish occasionally seems to help. The medical director distracts himself with stacks of pornographic "literature" and lends me some books to study; it's a vocabulary that I don't have yet, and another dissociative defense.

I tiptoe past the room where a man has tetanus—the only case I'll ever see. A sign outside his room reminds passersby to be silent. If he gets excited, lockjaw will choke him to death. But nobody needs a sign to remember to be quiet. Everybody is *always* quiet in the hospital. All conversations are in whispers. It's not safe to be heard. Any stated or implied moral or political opinion or stance whatsoever means that *somebody*, in at least one of the fractious factions, would find reason to "disappear" you. **Shhh!** One must keep quiet and be invisible to avoid human predation.

A typical clinic day…

I console the mother of a stillborn fetus. I hang up plastic disposable gloves on a clothesline to dry in the sun and re-use. A nursing mother comes to me with a huge breast abscess. The only antibiotic available is penicillin, and that probably won't work. I don't have endotracheal tubing for the general anesthesia machine yet, and there is no local anesthesia such as lidocaine. One of the doctors hands me a scalpel and tells me, *"Just do it."* I stab deep into the petrified woman's breast; she jolts back, fighting me and howling in pain as milk, pus, and blood pour out of the gaping wound.

At night, there is a bat problem…

The largest room in the hospital is the morgue. I am possessed by a strange thought: Am I delirious to imagine that the number of bats that hover and hang in the rafters of the open-air corridors is equal to the number of dead in the morgue?

One morning the hospital janitor, who is usually a cheerful woman in her forties, stands sobbing at my door. She tells me that her father was a very respected man in town, an honorable man, a good man. All he did was to try to organize a labor union for the workers. He should have known better. He's in the hospital and five bullets are in his neck.

I go to see the patriarch. He's alert, trying to smile although half of his mouth is blown off. He's in terrible pain, and needs urgent reconstructive oral-facial-maxillary surgery to survive. All I can do is suction fluids from his penetrating wounds. He finally asphyxiates, drowning on his own blood a couple of days later.

The night the assassinated patriarch dies, a diseased bat without sonar flies directly toward my eyes and scratches wildly at my face. I run to my room in terror. I'm hyperventilating and cold as ice.

MICHAEL HOLLOWAY KING

My mother screams, "I should kill you now and take you out of your misery!"
She lunges at me with her fingers deformed into talons, scratching at my face.

I take a few hits of hashish and nitrous oxide and lock the door. That's when I develop a lifelong phobia about bats. When I watched the movie *Ghost* I cringed at the scenes where one of the "bad guys" is killed and a horde of screeching bat-like creatures descends upon his astral body to carry his soul away. I won't be able to watch the movie screen and I will walk out of the theater trembling.

The overhead fan is gradually becoming more unfastened to the ceiling. It wobbles erratically as the menacing blades turn around and around above me. I just stare at it in an out of body dream state of semi-consciousness.

Again, and again, I try to trace the ever-expanding elements that pose a potential risk. I wrack my brains to make sense of it all yet again. I review what little I know: While fighting among themselves, the guerrillas primarily avenge the injustice of slavery by punishing the rich plantation lords, with kidnappings, extortion, and sometimes murder. The plantation lords fund thousands of paramilitary assassins who attack the guerrillas and murder the workers and any identified "leftist" or "liberal" in the town, especially those who protest about their conditions or try to unionize.

The *right-wing* military cannot succeed in dismantling the three *left-wing* guerrilla groups, which are well hidden in the impenetrable mountainous jungle, nor can they curb the well-funded *ultra-right-wing* paramilitaries. After sustaining heavy losses, the military apparently decided to change their tactics: Publically campaigning for law and order and justice, the military places bounties on the heads of the paramilitary leaders. Then, they secretly *supply* those same paramilitary leaders with arms and free helicopter transportation to fight the guerrillas.

The paramilitary assassins are called *macetos*, or "mallet men." They often favor bludgeoning their victims to death with mallets to save their bullets. These henchmen are so skilled at "doing the dirty work" that they will be flown across the entire country, with hit lists provided by the military, to massacre whole families and towns of liberals.

But, like the military, the paramilitary militias are also failing to oust the guerrillas from the surrounding jungles. So, both the military and the paramilitary have decided it is easier to cut off the *supply line* to them: They torture and murder all suspicious civilians of Apartadó instead. That's when Apartadó was dubbed "The Killing fields of Colombia," home of arguably the worst terrorism in the world, lasting scores of decades and funded by American corporations.

Nobody can count the number of murders, so many tens or hundreds of thousands. But sadly, the children know. Graphic examples of neoslavery, reinforced by horrible acts of violence, are etched into the minds of many thousands of orphaned children who "saw" exactly how their parents and teenage siblings were dragged out of their shacks, raped, dismembered, and clubbed or shot to death. The littlest children are spared death; they are pulled outside to line up, watch the atrocities ... and learn, instead.

The more I try to understand the violence, the more variables appear. I revisit my stoner friend and eventually he tells me something that I promise to keep secret. There is a new export from Colombia: *cocaine*. A drug-lord named "Pablo Escobar" rules a cocaine cartel in Medellín and is becoming very rich and powerful. The route of export from Medellín connects to Apartadó by a tortuous road and by air. And Apartadó connects to Panama across the Bay of Urubá.

He tells me that a man named Manuel Noriega in Panama takes charge of the next stage: The cocaine flies to America on aircraft, possibly owned by, or cleared by, the CIA. Billions of dollars are being split among all three parties: the cartel, Noriega, and the CIA. Escobar is also about to "purchase" the presidency of Colombia and the divided loyalty of the military. He will pay the guerillas to not ambush the cocaine-loaded vehicles and to guarantee safe passage by land to Apartadó. He will also pay the paramilitaries to eradicate the guerillas. My friend thinks he knows what the CIA is doing with the drug money.

The CIA has yet another source of income: selling weapons to Iran. Thus, I am informed of news that will take a decade to be revealed to the American public. The Colombian drug cartels are just getting up to their full momentum while I am here...Pablo Escobar connects to Manuel Noriega, Noriega to the CIA, and the CIA to the Iran-Contra scandal of 1986 under President Reagan. The weapons sales will help release American hostages, after making President Carter look bad, to keep the Republicans looking good and in power for upcoming elections.

The money that the CIA gets from selling arms to Iran—and, if what my friend says is true, further income from abetting the trafficking of cocaine in America—will be used to fund the Contras, another paramilitary assassin group, to overthrow the left-wing Sandinista government in Nicaragua.

I am stuck in the middle of Cocaine Alley—the "Pablo Escobar Highway." Perhaps it's because I am beginning to put the pieces together, or because I'm an American or black or overheard talking "liberal," the time finally comes for the spotlight to turn on me and expose my invisibility. It's toward the end of my fourth month at the hospital.

An officer knocks on my door and tells me that I have two "very important visitors" waiting to chat with me at the little coffee stand outside the hospital gates. I notice the fretful expressions of the hospital staff as I walk outside to a table where a man in a suit and another in a decorated military uniform are seated.

"Would you like something to drink?" the military officer asks.

"I'll have an espresso, *double*."

"Let us introduce ourselves. I am the *Chief Commander* of the *Anti-paramilitary* units. My friend here is the *editor* of the local newspaper. We just want to interview you and ask you a few questions," the officer explains. I instantly know they're lying: The "Chief Commander" is either supporting the paramilitary units or he is a paramilitary officer, and the "editor" is a wealthy right-wing rancher.

The commander continues. "We find it strange that an *American* should appear here at this moment. As you know, there are very serious problems faced by the people of this town. There are some sensitive operations being carried out. What do you think about all that?"

His eyes are squinting, even under the shade of the umbrella over the table. The silent man in a suit has his arms crossed over his chest; he is leaning back on his tilted chair and staring at me with a deep frown.

"I don't know what you're talking about, sir. I'm just a last-year medical student learning about tropical medicine. Harvard has been sending students to this hospital for the past ten years." My nervous voice is getting squeaky and higher-pitched, and it's a challenge to be diplomatic in Spanish.

The officer turns to the expensively dressed man and says, "Make a note of that—Harvard knew that these operations were going to occur ten years ago." But the "newspaper editor" isn't taking any notes at all. He tilts his chair farther back with his arms still crossed over his chest. I feel shocked, threatened, and speechless. This "interview" is a set-up and I can see where it's going.

Suddenly, I have a flashback to Haiti seven years before:

"I passed the tests so far…. The 'interview' yesterday—
With a military-clad man whose look felt like a knife slitting my throat.
Was he one of the Tontons Macoutes?"

The officer clears his throat. "OK. So, tell me about your school—

Harvard. Would you say it's a liberal school?"

"Well, yes. I've had a liberal arts education and Harvard tends to be liberal." THE MACETO'S MALLET POUNDS THE DESK THE FIRST TIME...

"What, then, is your position on labor and unions?"

I don't know why I must tell the truth. An explosive, suppressed rage burns inside my chest. I sit up straight, lean far over the table, staring directly at the man in the suit. I regain my voice and the full clarity of my thoughts. "I believe that *all* workers deserve to have rights and to enjoy the profits of their labor. I believe that labor unions are essential in Apartadó because of the atrocious conditions the workers suffer." THE MACETO'S MALLET SLAMS DOWN THE SECOND TIME...

I continue, suddenly more fluent in Spanish than ever. "I am an African American and what I see here is equal to slavery, or worse. I hope that *you*—the so-called 'press'—and *you* there—the so-called 'military'—are aware that violence is not the answer. I deeply regret that so much of this is due to American money and its corporations." THE MACETO'S MALLET MARKS THREE TIMES...

'You're out!'

Thor's hammer has condemned me: I am in the *wrong* place at the *wrong* time. But I'm counting on my Ace cards. First, it would attract international attention if they tortured or killed me. Harvard would try to protect me and would protest loudly, and my interrogators know that. Second, I decide in that moment...*I am going to get the hell out of FUCKING CRAZY APARTADÓ on the first flight, either tomorrow or as soon as possible.*

When I return to Harvard Medical School, I give a full debriefing to my faculty, especially to Dieter Koch-Weiser, the previous Assistant Secretary General of the World Health Organization, in charge of all South American operations. He's surprised, but not shocked. I will be the last student to ever study "tropical medicine" in Apartadó. Harvard is powerless when compared to Pablo Escobar.

News from Apartadó occasionally reaches America. Not much news...it's so isolated and small compared to other hot spots in the world, which all share a similar misfortune. But it appears that nothing has changed. The Marxist guerrillas still control their zones and have the loyalty of the *neo*-enslaved, *un*-unionized workers.

Increasingly powerful paramilitary groups, apparently backed by the Colombian army and banana plantation owners, and funded by Chiquita Banana to "protect its financial interests," massacre thousands of innocent civilians every year. Chiquita has fully admitted to this, but only received a "slap on the wrist" fine by federal investigators.

Is the population of Apartadó brutalized to stop socialist-leaning movements that oppose the United States? Is it necessary to clear the highway route of "guerilla robbers" that could interfere with the trafficking of lucrative cocaine exports to America? Is the massacre of civilians necessary to protect the corporate interests of Chiquita Banana and Dole?

All three possibilities are American-made. But the "goods" are not made by America. And all three reasons for the bloodshed are entirely about protecting vested corporate interests and the concentration of wealth. Ultimately, these possibilities, or any *other* interpretation of events, are all about money.

Even today, I fail to put the pieces of the puzzle of Apartadó all together. So much is kept secret. Perhaps it's best that I stop trying to understand such violence and envision Apartadó as a truly "isolated" case: a mountain and jungle-encased *nowhere* that knows not the passage of time. Apartadó is just a sleepy, sweaty little city, which is as quiet as a morgue.

This is a journalistic exposé about medical murder, routinely inflicted on black patients in a community hospital.

IN-VOLUNTARY EUTHANASIA

The neurosurgery unit at Highland General Hospital is a busy place in 1982. As the only charity hospital serving the poor and predominantly African-American city of Oakland, California, it is flooded with indigent black patients. Conversely, almost all the physicians at the hospital are white. It's a training hospital, where interns become residents, and then a few become chief residents, but always under the complete rule of the attending physicians.

There are endless reasons that a patient would need neurosurgery or end up in the neurosurgery unit. Violence in the ghettoes of Oakland and its environs is among the highest in the nation, and gunshot wounds to the head or bludgeoning of the head are common. But there are also drunk drivers who sustain trauma to the head, or malnourished elderly women who fall on their head, and, perhaps the *majority*, comas due to drug overdoses. Most patients arrive in a coma and are put on respiratory life support to maintain their breathing. Technically, they're still "alive."

The highest level of respect for physicians is deeply entrenched in the surgical specialties, where Narcissism peaked in the early 1980s. And among all the surgical specialties, the brain surgeon is the unquestioned epitome of the "Gentleman Doctor," the magnificent Doctor Deity, who carries an aura of awe and omnipotence.

The attending physician of the unit, the absolute boss who arbitrarily sets the rules and customs of his domain, is a harsh and dogmatic middle-aged man. I now realize that he had a narcissistic personality. In truth, *most* surgeons who I have known have had narcissistic qualities, and narcissists assume automatic compliance to their expectations and orders.

Dr. Gaul has a system to evaluate his coma patients. Upon admission to the neurosurgery unit, they would each get an EEG, an *electroencephalogram*, to see if there is activity in the cortex of the brain. If the EEG reading were flat, indicating no higher cortical activity, they would be maintained on life support for one week. Then, they would get a second EEG. If it was *still* flat, Dr. Gaul and his residents, including myself as an intern on the service, engaged in an orchestrated ritual.

Dr. Gaul pulls the curtains around the comatose victim shut. He turns off the respirator. We all wait for about five minutes. When Dr. Gaul is certain that the patient is dead, the respirator is turned back on and the curtains are opened. A death certificate is signed, always the same: "Natural death due to head trauma, complicated by coma."

No outside opinions, no panel of peers, no ethics committee, *nobody* has a voice in Dr. Gaul's unilateral and dogmatic decision making. Under such rules, my sister-in-law, who suffered a *two*-week long coma from which she spontaneously and completed recovered, would be dead today.

No family member could enjoy a little more time with the comatose patient, to talk to him or her with the prayer that the words might somehow be heard, or to give their consent about the timing of the termination of their loved one's life.

The nurses in the unit, as do the physician residents, all know exactly what has happened. The nurses could rationalize the need to free up beds for the incessant onslaught of new head trauma patients. That's easier on their conscience than admitting they are pleased to have a lighter workload. The resident physicians go along because their future depends on pleasing the attending physician, the boss.

Like a dysfunctional family, we are all sworn to tacit approval and secrecy about the involuntary euthanasia. *Nobody* in the patient's outside world or family would know, *nobody* inside the neurosurgery department would tell, and, perhaps, *nobody* would ever care that what had just happened was—*murder.*

I was a mere intern, only passing through a rotation. But my shock and my conscience as a witness and passive bystander, more than an accomplice, felt stretched to a nearly unbearable breaking point. My guilt as a silent co-conspirator would last for the rest of my life and the murders still haunt me—but much less now that I have written the Truth.

I was only on the neurosurgery service for a one-month rotation; during that single month, I witnessed over half a dozen acts of "involuntary euthanasia." I cannot imagine, over the course of many years, how many patients have quietly been "disappeared." But one thing I did note was, besides having two flat EEGs one week apart, all the patients had two other things in common: They were all *poor* and they were all *black.*

At the same time, in a different city, back east in Erie, Pennsylvania, my father is the medical director of Lake Erie Extended Rehabilitation, a private hospital for comatose patients from wealthy families. Their bodies are flown to the hospital, where they will receive daily massages, physical therapy, nutritional supplementation, and wound care. They will be pampered and fretted over with exquisite and indefinite attention, perhaps *eternal* care—because they are *rich* and *white.*

A much more tragic and complex story of medical murder and physician brutality perpetrated on another African American...

THE PRETZEL MAN

I've come to like a black patient during my internship at Highland General Hospital. Perhaps not exactly "like," but at least establish rapport with him and hear his sad saga. He'd been a burglar and stole to maintain his costly cocaine habit. He was caught running from the police. They shot him in the back. He became a paraplegic and lost movement and sensation from his bellybutton down.

That all happened five years ago, and now he is in the hospital because of huge erosions of his buttocks, called *Decubitus ulcers.* He'd spent too much time sitting in his wheelchair and could not feel the sensations that we all experience, telling us to shift our weight. His left buttock is rotten and gone; it's a concave pit instead of a convex cheek. Every day, I turn him on his side and treat the wound, snipping out dead tissue and debris, and then filling it with fresh gauze. It was very slowly healing.

But the chief surgical resident has an idea to fix the patient's wound quickly; he wants to do an original operation and write an article about it. He plans to graft and fuse the useless right *foot* directly onto the left *buttock*. They are the same size. With the leg and foot permanently twisted up, back, and behind the man, the chief jokes that the paraplegic will end up "looking like a pretzel." The residents all laugh at the thought: "He'll literally have his *foot* in his *ass!*"

The chief resident is a very angry and scary man. More than once, I've seen him smiling when a post-op patient codes and the chief instantly takes a huge scalpel, hatchets the patient's chest wide open through the sternum, and rips out the heart to do "open cardiac massage." It's like an Aztec sacrifice on the sacred stone atop a pyramid. Once, he ordered me to keep manually pumping the heart of a dead man and simulate blood flow for hours and hours, until my hand went into spastic exhaustion. That was just for the chief to practice arterial reconstruction of the dead man's legs.

Nobody crosses the chief resident. He's the interim boss of general surgery because the *real* chief of surgery has been fired in a sexual harassment case filed by a female African-American resident. Thus, there exists nobody above the chief resident and he can do whatever he likes.

But the soon-to-be "pretzel patient" is very depressed; he hardly eats and is too wasted away to survive such a major operation. It's necessary to fatten him up first. The chief has determined that he should receive nasogastric tube feedings for hyper-alimentation, but my patient doesn't want a thick tube in his nose. He refuses both hyper-alimentation *and* the pretzel surgery.

My supervising resident has an idea: *bribe him.*

Pharmaceutical-quality cocaine in liquid form is ordered and the patient receives an "extra-large dose" under the pretext of anesthetizing his nose to pass the NG tube. In fact, he receives an "extra-large dose" of cocaine at least twice a day, until...

I'm just an intern, but I am smart enough to see that a psychiatrist has placed the patient on lithium. The thick, tubal hyper-alimentation begins to produce diarrhea. The patient becomes dehydrated and the lithium level I order shows it is twice the upper limits of normal. The *lethal* dose of lithium is twice the upper limits of normal, at which time the heart stops beating.

I rush to tell the chief resident, who yells at me, "Shut up, you're just an intern." Surgeons are the extreme antipode of psychiatrists and they look down on such a sissy, feely specialty. Besides, the chief is adamantly determined to do his pretzel operation the next day.

By the next day, it's too late. My patient has a cardiac arrest and is whisked to the surgical intensive care unit. The chief surgeon is furious with his patient. When the paraplegic's heart stops for the last time, the chief pounds his clenched fists on the dying man's chest. He pounds much harder than what is approved of for a last resort in cardiac arrest. Then, the chief resident pounds again and again, *harder and harder,* until the ribs are cracking. *"DAMN YOU!"* he shouts into the dying man's ears.

The blows and the curse will be the last sensations and words my patient's soul will experience on Earth. The chief resident's experimental surgery and his publishable paper are ruined. We will all keep the reason for the death a secret.

The chief resident frightens us all.

Very few doctors have had an experience such as this—working in San Quentin Prison during a time of extreme unrest, gang violence including the Aryan Brotherhood, and in risk of one's life. There are comedic elements included, and revelation of the truth inside of the criminal justice system stands out in stark detail.

WHISTLE WHILE YOU WORK

I flee from Napa State Hospital and arrive at San Quentin amidst its most violent recorded phase in history. I think that the aftermath of "Black August" —August 21, 1971—has passed, but I'm wrong. That was when black militant writer and author of "Soledad Brother," political prisoner, George Jackson, was set up for assassination during a rebellion in which three prison guards were killed.

Concessions were made to improve conditions for inmates beginning a decade later, and they included better access to medical care—unrestricted and unguarded access to the doctor.

I "look good."

I am a token black doctor and a Harvard-trained doctor.

And I'd signed the "no hostage release" statement as a condition of employment: If I were taken hostage, there would be no effort whatsoever to rescue me.

On my first day, the chief warden takes me into his private trophy room. Inside is a museum that displays the hundreds of weapons that have been confiscated from the prisoners. Even newspapers have been rolled into sturdy spears, capable of lethal piercing from afar. Next, I'm escorted to the electric chair and told to get ready; I'd have to do a full medical exam to make sure that the convict was in perfect health just before he was killed.

This is a restless time at the prison.

"Lock Down" occurs every two or three days.

Riots are commonplace.

Gang wars between the blacks, the Aryan Brotherhood, the Italian and the Mexican mafias, and all their sub-divided factions produce an atmosphere of terror. An attempted murder happens twice a week; a successful murder of an inmate happens every couple of weeks. The guards have been issued Mini-14 target rifles; I think they were called that because they leave an exit hole fourteen inches in diameter. One shot, and the whole shoulder is gone.

A fear of death envelops the prison. As I walk through the concrete yards where all but those scheduled for execution could exercise or mingle, I find myself muttering, "Yea, though I walk through the valley of the shadow of death, I fear no evil, for Thou art with me…." I comfort myself with an image and a phrase: "A *speck* of light is a *beacon* in the vortex of evil."

Part of my job is to do sick call in an eight-by-eight-foot metal shack that used to be a barbershop, located in the center of West Block's concrete yard. There, I am completely alone, unassisted and face-to-face with my patients. I have the sole option to sit behind a metallic desk; I'm grateful for the desk because nobody can see my legs trembling or hear my knees knocking together.

The prisoners come by the dozens, one gang at a time. The Aryan Brotherhood lines up. The group originated in the prison and then expanded nationwide. A huge man with swastika and teardrop tattoos approaches the desk where I am seated. The number of teardrops indicates the number of people he has murdered; professional assassins stop after five teardrops or so because they run out of space on their cheeks.

The Aryan Brotherhood prisoner thrusts a clenched right fist to within a millimeter from my face. I can see the knuckles are bleeding, calloused, and raw. When I offer to treat the wounds, the prisoner spoke. "I don't want them treated. I want more acid to pour on them. *The pain makes me feel alive and reminds me how much I hate niggers.*"

I have a strategic ally in the prison with whom I feel safe. Nurse Sherry has two careers: nursing and being a pin-up porn star. She is demure and soft-spoken when we have an opportunity to do rounds together. Her low-cut blouse and enormous breasts are tantalizing. Most of the inmates have photographs of her from Playboy or other magazines hanging up in their cells.

And they will do *anything* she asks.

A very large Great Dane accompanies Sherry when she goes jogging from her nearby home. When she notices that a former inmate, released on probation, is stalking her, she subtly deviates from Route A to Route B, where the latter passes by the local police department. She goes inside to chat with her friends there and casually adds in parting, "Oh, and by the way, Christopher Higgins is violating his parole and stalking me. You wouldn't mind picking him up for me, would you?" She resumes her jogging. Sherry is used to being stalked. The parolee is promptly returned to prison.

Sherry becomes my security blanket and my best friend.

This is one of the days when the warden is giving a tour to agents of the press. He is making a point of demonstrating the complete accessibility of inmate medical care; that means *me* in my little shack. What the press does not know is that, unlike anybody else in the prison, the two or three physicians are completely exposed to prisoners without any protection. Unlike the job rehab counselors, the ministers, or *any* visitor, volunteer, or employee, including all the other medical personnel—such as psychiatrists, dentists, and nurses—we are not allowed guarded protection.

The reason is never explained to me.

I smile and seem to please the reporters. But I scarcely utter half a sentence before the warden cuts me off and quickly pushes the entourage of photographers and journalists outside and onwards to the next stop on the tour. He doesn't want me to say anything that might taint the image he is inventing for the press. As the warden is leaving last, I quietly call him back for the only opportunity I'll ever have in nearly a year to talk to him. I whisper one sentence about my terror of the long lines of unsupervised, unguarded, level four prisoners, which means serial killers or worse, walking freely right up to my face.

I don't have time to describe all the threats and seductions, or the fact that the prisoners somehow know every detail about me—where I live, that I am living with a man, and even the arrangement of my furniture. I do not have time to tell him that I'd just discovered that something was being stowed in a secret pocket in the trunk of my car, and most probably it was being smuggled inside.

The chief warden whispers back, "Here, take my whistle. When a prisoner assaults you, *blow it*. The two sentry guards up there on the second floor, protected behind a dome of bulletproof glass, will fire a single round of blind shots into your metal shack through the one small window and the door—if it's open. The bullets will ricochet about eight times and end up wherever they happen to lodge, either in the desk, the walls, the inmate, or you." He gives me a gold whistle and resumes smiling and impressing the press agents, showing them "only the best."

Nine months later, I quit the job after cracking two molars from gritting my teeth.

This somewhat long excerpt represents the climax of "Hide and Play Dead" and reveals the abusive, slave-like and racist conditions within the medical field. Again, the flashback phrases may not all be familiar to the reader who has not read the original book, but one can imagine the scenarios they depict.

IT TAKES TWO TO TANGLE

My temp job agent calls and tells me that an opportunity has just opened in Marin County, at the community clinic organization there. I love Marin! It's natural beauty with forests and beaches, its liberal and educated population, its proximity to San Francisco...

It's even the county with the most per capita billionaires in the world. Yet, it also has a huge poverty-stricken underclass, comprised of immigrants who work for the rich and the recently unemployed. This is especially true, since the recession has just hit hard, affecting primarily the poorest northern sector of the county where I'd be stationed.

My interview is typically brief. The chief medical officer, Dr. Furie, is the "head honcho" manager of all the physicians in the chain of clinics. She is a cold, drab, and humorless woman in her late fifties. I cannot bond with her; she seems to dislike my open and enthusiastic personality.

Dr. Furie grills me, and then condemns me. "You're *under*-qualified because you don't have board eligibility in internal medicine." I point out that studies have shown that the higher the board exam scores, the *poorer* the patient outcomes, and that my vast clinical experience of thirty years must have *some* value. She frowns and says, "But it's a *policy*. Perfect credentials matter to physicians in *this* county!"

Then I meet the next in the chain of physician command, the clinic site's medical director, who is the only adult medicine physician in the clinic, Dr. Leery. He is an exceedingly tall, skinny man in his early forties. "Your CV is the most *interesting* I've ever seen!" he raves. Dr. Leery does all the talking, which is fast and tangential, filled with abstruse mumbled words. He says that he'd like to include complementary medicine in the practice and I'd be an asset.

I demonstrate a way to establish instant rapport, enacting a hypnotic technique I'd invented to reduce spinal pain and boost a patient's self-esteem at the same time—all in less than a few minutes. "As far as I'm concerned, you're *over*-qualified and you're hired!" Dr. Leery announces, and his vote trumps Dr. Furie's.

My pay is the same as it has always been for the past twenty to thirty years: Seventy dollars per contracted hour, with some benefits. I would be scheduled to see a patient every fifteen minutes and there are "quotas." I am contracted to work part-time, twenty-eight hours per week. When I ask if there is an opportunity to work a few more hours per week, I receive a strange look from Dr. Furie. "*Nobody* has ever worked here more than part-time. *It's impossible.*"

Dr. Leery gives me a ten-minute orientation briefing on my first day of work. He appears irritated about taking the time from his more important duties. He offers no information about vital community resources or specialized computer and Internet support systems; he likes to keep *his* information a secret.

Slowly, the sordid truth about my two superiors and the special history of the clinic site emerge like a vampire arising from his casket. My dream job turns into the worst nightmare of my working career.

With the clinic's floodgates always open to more revenue from new patients, the full original caseload that had burnt out almost *twenty* physicians in the three years before my arrival will *quadruple* within the next six months. Soon, I am responsible for five hundred critical care patients, over two thousand chronic care patients, and ten to twenty complex new patients scheduled to see me every day.

The recent immigrants from Third World countries pose extra problems of illiteracy, language barriers, and nil prior medical care. They have no medical insurance whatsoever, and all are charity cases. Most of the American-born patients are frail, demented, homeless, and drug-addicted, as well as demanding. The prevalence of untreated and severe mental illness is astronomical, and the organization's psychiatrist just resigned in exhaustion before I arrive. 'It's a good thing that I'm experienced in mental health!' I think.

The average patient has three acute problems, often life threatening, and a litany of sub-acute, dangerous, and chronic problems. Just to write down all their problems would take up the allotted fifteen minutes. The no-show rate drops to zero and the community clinic is rapidly becoming an intensive care medical center.

"THAT'S A LIE!" My superiors accuse me of fabricating statistics about the volume and complexity of my caseload. But the entire staff knows it is true.

The only prior physician, who'd lasted in my position for more than a few months, working just two days a week, is also a Harvard Medical School graduate; she only lasted eight months. She occasionally comes back, but just for half-day shifts a couple of times a month.

Like me, she needs the money.

When she realizes that the demand to see *more* patients has soared, and the critical level of illness has risen to the level of disaster, she breaks down and becomes hysterical.

She screams in front of the staff, "THIS IS PHYSICIAN ABUSE!" Before she left for good, she whispers to me in fear of the management overhearing her words, "The only way to survive here, Michael, is to pack your schedule with as many easy return visits as possible."

One physician has been tough enough to stay with the organization for the entire twenty-five years of her working life as a doctor, but with special arrangements to *only* see new patients, *once*, and delegate the complex on-going care to other doctors.

She warns me: "You've got fifteen minutes to do *everything* for a patient. So you've got to be rude! Hammer out the basic information with uninterrupted questions. Tell them you can only perhaps address *one* current problem and all the other problems, life-threatening or not, will require many return visits. Don't let them know that your schedule is booked solid for three months. And never ask them about their emotional problems—*they're all in crisis.*" She continues, emphatically, "After five minutes face-to-face, tell them all, 'TIME'S UP.' *And then, just walk out the door.*"

She, too, fears the management, especially the site's medical director, Dr. Leery. She says that he is worse than cruel, controlling, and paranoid: He's *dangerous.* "That's the real reason nobody stays here, Michael," the doctor explains. "They feel totally unsupported by him. Furthermore, this is by far the hardest site. It has the poorest, sickest patients, ranging from those locked in homes for the mentally retarded to end-stage geriatrics. Almost none of them are English-speaking, none have ever had routine medical care until near death, which is when they finally come in."

Like almost all doctors, Drs. Leery and Furie don't know how to be managers. They've had no management training or interest in managing—at least, not in the sense of supporting, motivating, and guiding people. They just rule their lesser physicians with arbitrary mandates. Together, they practice the old guard style of management that still exists in the military, in totalitarian systems, and in dictatorships: "Do as I say, or you're fired." And every day, I lived with the fear that I would be fired, for *no* reason or for *any* reason at all.

Fortunately, I rarely see Dr. Furie. "I came by to see how you are doing, but you were with a patient," she says and then walks off. But I am *always* with a patient, nonstop and running. Dr. Leery terrifies me and I look forward to the days he's not in the clinic at the same time with me. He is feared and loathed by the staff, but he doesn't seem to mind or even notice. Whenever he enters the break room, all jovial conversation abruptly stops as everyone shifts to a tense silence.

During morning report, a circle of twenty to thirty staff members gathers at one of the nursing station counters. They all leave a wide and conspicuous breach around Dr. Leery; nobody wants to stand near him. He leans, lording and lurching over the counter as he stares at the clinic manager to establish dominance over her. Then he suddenly picks on an employee for unpredictable humiliation in front of the staff.

One day, he lectures me about how to show empathy and establish rapport. "All you need to do is make direct eye contact for about ten seconds." He then *glares* at me for ten seconds and I feel acutely ill at ease. Dr. Leery has never had a management position before; I am the only employee that he manages, and he knows only one way to manage. "I have to be the *police dog* here. I hate doing it, I'm not good at it, but that's how it is," he declares.

Any educated professional who could expose Dr. Leery's errors has either been demoted to powerlessness or summarily let go. I learn that any disagreement with him, the *slightest* sign of opposition, merits the same fate.

One morning, I hear the two most experienced nurses wailing in shock and I rush over to console them; they'd just been laid off without notice after many years of service. They had also sometimes disagreed with Dr. Leery. The only nurse that is permitted to remain has only six months of experience as an RN; being inexperienced and scared, she does not pose a risk. She just obeys orders.

The *clinic manager* has been here for only six months, too; the previous one had been fired for being "too nice." She describes the staff's morale upon her arrival as "the lowest I've ever seen in my thirty years in medicine." The low morale is blamed on her predecessor's "niceness." But the manager slowly realizes that it is due to Dr. Leery's "meanness."

The political alliance between my two medical superiors slowly becomes apparent. In meetings with them, intended to check in with me, I feel like a mere shadow of an inferior nothing. I am a slave-child in the master's house, "To be seen, but not heard." I watch as Dr. Leery overwhelms Dr. Furie with rapid-fire phrases and abstractions until she falls into a hypnotic trance. Then he embeds his own agenda in her mind. They have a bond, which is called *folie a deux*, because they share the same delusions.

They are an inseparable unit of abiding mutual loyalty.

Dr. Leery's charts are full of scribbles that are as readable as Chinese characters. He claims he has a "writing disorder" and has obtained the special privilege of dictating his notes. That way, he can cover himself; if something is not perfectly right, he can alter the dictation or blame the transcriptionist before it goes on record.

A nearly comatose patient of Dr. Leery appears in the clinic. Her son says she'd taken an overdose of some of her long list of twenty medications. He doesn't know what medications his mother has been prescribed by Dr. Leery. "It's in the chart!" he declares in exasperation, like so many patients who imagine that a medical chart is organized or of any use at all. I panic, trying to decipher the notes on the chart and the copies of cryptic prescriptions. I end up sending the woman to the ER for a toxicology screen, without any history. The ER doc chastises me for sending him a bogus patient; she was feigning to get attention, manipulate her son, and upset and disrupt the medical staff "just for fun." But I had to chart the truth: The medications and history were unknown due to my inability to read the medical records.

After the staff is gone, and when there are no witnesses, Dr. Leery suddenly appears looming over my desk. "How *dare* you write that my notes are illegible in the chart of a patient! You're exposing me and plan to ruin my career!"

I have inadvertently become his archenemy.

One month later, Dr. Leery suddenly appears again when there is nobody left working except for me. He wants a private *tête-à-tête* about "how things are going." It's the first time my only colleague, my superior, has offered to talk with me. He puts me in an exam room after scanning the empty hallway and closes the door firmly. Then he sits down on the single chair in the room while I stand "at attention" against a wall. I have only a moment to say that I feel overwhelmed by the flood of so many complex, new patients.

"Of course you're overwhelmed!" Dr. Leery scoffs. "*First*, the effects of the recession have suddenly hit and the doors here are wide open without limits to new patients that will all fall in your lap.

"*Second*, you're new to both the job and the patients and it will take at least six months to learn how to do this job—you're just in your third month. But by then, you'll have to learn a new system of electronic medical records and you'll have many more new patients to deal with, so you're *stuck*.

"*Third*, the patients are non-English speaking and very, very complex, with insatiable demands and expectations.

"*Fourth*, you are in a solo practice here and because we don't generate a profit on charity cases, you won't ever get any support or adequate staffing.

"*Fifth*, your caseload was already full when you arrived, and over twice the national average, filled with patients who are virtual train wrecks.

"*Sixth*...." He curtly lists more and more reasons why I should be overwhelmed, with no offer to remedy the crisis.

At the end, he adds without any change in his droning and rattling voice, as if it were an ultimate condemnation: "Besides, you are practicing good medicine, not just placating one problem per visit! You must stop trying to get the big picture of a patient. You will gradually, over years, *maybe* put it together. That style of holism, that ideal of seeing how to cure from getting all the information, putting together a comprehensive plan, and treating the whole patient is...*GONE!*"

I timidly interrupt the monologue.

I ask him if he'd help me see some of the mushrooming influx of new patients, since he's now *privately* admitted that my caseload was already full since the day I started. He instantly becomes berserk and ballistic. He arches backwards with his eyebrows raised and his forehead deeply creased. His thunderous voice is accompanied with slapping gestures on his thighs to silence me.

"*That's preposterous!* You're out of line to ask *me* to help *you!* You're my *inferior* and you must earn the right to have a closed practice like I have. It will take *years* to acquire my level of seniority and my political connections!" He adds with a sarcastic tone, "Maybe, *THEN*, you'll have the power I have. Maybe, *THEN*, you won't have to work so hard. Maybe, *THEN*, you'll have the special privileges that I have. Maybe, *THEN*, you can have an easy and familiar caseload like I have!"

Dr. Leery now appears unpredictably and more often, even cornering me during the daytime in front of staff. One evening, when it's already after closing hour and I still have several of my own patients waiting to be seen for urgent problems, he stomps up to me at the nursing station. He shrieks, "You will see one of *my* patients, *NOW!* I've finished *my* workday and I'm going home."

I am treated like a slave and I feel like a slave to his dictates.

One of the medical assistants warns me, "*Never* interrupt Dr. Leery! He becomes furious if you knock on his door when he's with a patient." I am not brave enough to ask for any support until I'm desperate for a second opinion. One day, I must knock at his door for advice about a non-healing wound. When Dr. Leery finally comes over to look at my patient, he barks out a mixed bitter salad of insults and orders…

"How *stupid* to use that dressing, KING! Stop that wound care treatment, *now!*" He storms off without giving any suggestion as to what I *should* do instead, mumbling like a wild turkey cursing me.

One former medical assistant is now in medical school. She is being paid to come back for a week to "*whip* the other medical assistants into shape." She hears and watches Dr. Leery berate and humiliate me at the nursing station. "I worked here for three years," she moans. "Every day, Dr. Leery beat me down like that. Every day, I assumed that he *hated* me. At the end, I had to ask him for a recommendation for medical school, and he praised me. I nearly fainted from the surprise."

*

Despite the hardships, I loved helping the patients and I stay.

I weave myself into the work. I learn to shortcut the systems of vital computerized databases and I become an expert in the management of rare and emerging diseases. I establish rapport with the orneriest patients. I hear their tragic stories—the traumatic exposure to near-death, domestic abuse, and violent warfare that almost all the immigrants bring with them as refugees from their homeland. I prevent suicides and give my patients hope, education, and motivation to get well or stay alive.

A typical day at the clinic is so far beyond the scope of an ordinary, "usual and customary" medical practice as to leave any physician in shock, and any *non*-physician observer changed for life. All my skills are desperately needed and no other doctor in the chain of three clinics has such skills. My knowledge about shame is invaluable. My ability to reach deeply into the patient's emotional core and the true sources of their physical disease works miracles.

Patients tell me that the reputation of the clinic was abysmal before I arrived. Soon after I started working at the clinic, adult medicine began to enjoy a good reputation for the first time. Most of my patients also tell me that I am the first doctor in their whole lives to listen to them, help them, and in most cases, cure them of serious problems. I become the most effective and popular doctor in all the organization's history.

The nursing director lauds me. "I constantly hear patients boasting about having you as their doctor. The talk fills the waiting room!" Patients enter the exam room in tears and leave with light-hearted laughter. Every morning, I take time to personally greet each member of the staff and morale soars. The staff brings their own family members to see me.

And I receive gifts in return. There are the countless notes of appreciation and gratitude. Flowers and presents fill my office. Patients praise me in emergency rooms and in the hospitals and by word of mouth to their friends and neighbors. Priests and pastors laud me in their sermons and support me by name in their prayers.

But there is a limit to human adaptability.

For over nine months, I work so hard that I have no time to eat, use the bathroom, or wash my hands between patients. I rarely get any sleep. My work hours last until midnight and through every weekend. My caseload mushrooms from full to infinity without any endpoint. I am working ninety unpaid extra hours every week, and my hourly pay drops to less than twenty dollars.

My two superiors do not appreciate the gifts I bring to the clinic and envy the gifts that I receive. It's only a matter of *money* for the management. But it's a matter of life or death for my patients, and I choose to give them life.

Then it becomes a matter of life or death for me…

I develop hypertension; my EKG shows signs of early heart disease and I begin fainting. I am always dehydrated and starving. I am exhausted beyond burnout. I begin to wonder if a death note revealing the labor abuse and the crisis at the clinic would be helpful when I killed myself.

"It is estimated that half a million slaves were used to build the fortress and their life expectancy was only three years. When they could not work anymore, they were thrown into these crocodile pits for amusement."

After six months, a search for an extra physician finally begins. But I discover that the objective is not to reduce my workload, but to further increase the patient volume. One doctor is hired and he's about my age. He lasts two weeks on the job, and then he has a heart attack. He never returns.

Another MD stays for six weeks. She protests that the workload and gravity of the illnesses are the worst she has encountered in forty years. After her protest, she is let go. Her voice is choking and tears stream down her cheeks as she is escorted by security to the exit.

My two superiors focus on me with suspicion; I've become too popular and I know too much now. I must to be discredited, for the truth could embarrass them. I am Chicken Little.

"I'M A THREAT!"

After the clinic closes for the weekend, and, once again, when nobody is left in the building as a witness, Dr. Leery leans back in his special-order, colossal easy chair and glares at me. I am putting on my hat, just about to leave, exhausted. He points to a small pile of charts that I have not had time to review yet. Then he yells, "So, what's *UP* with those charts there?"

"I'm sorry. I plan to finish them over the weekend. I'll work overtime to do it," I meekly reply.

"*WHAT?* I don't *get* this overtime," he screams. "You don't get overtime. I get paid *administrative* time to do my charts. You don't get *anything*. You're just an employee!"

"You're just a nigger slave boy!"

I begin to cry. The tears seem to encourage him to insult me further. I don't remember what follows, but I know I bowed my head in submissive silence, and when he finished with me, I left.

"He penetrates me without warning, thrusting a hot iron that pierces my virgin anus. The pain is unbearable and I start to cry."

The next Monday, Dr. Leery finds himself alone in what had been a shared office together. I call human resources and file a grievance. The entire staff is behind me, and all begin to come forth with their nightmares of being harassed, ridiculed, and threatened by Dr. Leery. Yet, they cower when Dr. Furie appears in the clinic to quell the rebellion. Her presence aborts morale like a condemned man watching the henchman approach the gallows. She'd earned the nickname "The Evil Empress," and Dr. Leery was called "Darth Vader."

I am summoned to meet with Dr. Furie. "Well, you've moved to a separate office. I've allowed HR to investigate it. I hereby *order* you to get along with Dr. Leery!" Dr. Furie spits the words out between clenched teeth.

I said I feared Dr. Leery shows signs of paranoia. That's the moment that I slit my throat. I'd just done the unforgivable—I'd exposed the ultimate truth about her closest ally. Dr. Furie flies into a vicious assault, saying that even such a *thought* was inappropriate and unacceptable, and that unless I instantly dropped the complaint and obeyed her...

There is a long pause as she scowls at me. My tongue is stuck to the dry roof of my mouth and I can barely find my voice. I try to break the red-hot iron of hate. I ask Dr. Furie how she thinks the meeting is going. She retorts with a desultory tone, "Well, what do *you* think?" Then she abruptly ends the five-minute meeting. "I've taken valuable time during a flu epidemic to meet with you and you should be grateful." Her index finger points to the door.

My grievance is archived as the medical management orders the investigation be suspended. I must now try to "be a good boy." I backtrack in humble subservience. I promise to do everything possible to connect with Dr. Leery. I suggest to Dr. Leery that we check in regularly, before morning report, to discuss my most difficult patients and get his advice. 'It will flatter his ego and reduce his paranoia,' I think.

I placate Dr. Leery's will and compliment him often. I pretend to be stupid. I never disagree with him again, even though many of his statements and ideas are patently paranoid and crazy. I stand next to him in morning report. He's aware that he has just barely escaped a full staff-wide mutiny; so, he now asks me to punish the rebels. He has a hit list of culprits. I am told to document how lazy and incompetent these employees are, and to gather condemning evidence on the selected targets...

It is now nine months since I started working and I have broken the longest tenure on record. Dr. Leery finally gives me my six-month probationary period evaluation. It's his chance to avenge the real traitor—*me*. He interviews staff to find something negative to report about me, *anything* negative, but only praise is uncovered. Many staff members simply refuse to fill out forms designed to disclose my faults. "Why do *you* have to be evaluated by *him?* We've never been allowed to evaluate him. Man, we'd have a *lot* to say about his behavior!" a flustered medical assistant laments.

Dr. Leery begins his evaluation of my performance. "The staff *seems* to like you. But they complain that you spend too much time with patients and slow down the flow. Your chart notes and updating of problem lists and medications are exemplary. You are brilliant and anyone would assume that you've done two fellowships in advanced areas of internal medicine. *But you are failing to adjust to the current practice of healthcare in America.*"

Dr. Leery has carefully been collecting my charts and chosen only a few with very detailed notes on terribly complex patients. He has shown these to Dr. Furie and used his influence to convince her that my triple and quadruple hours are all due to "excessive thoroughness." It is a convenient ruse, a disclaimer, and a way to finally justify … I am "bad" for being "too good."

"And—that's not good for business."

Perhaps as an African-American and the only black physician in the organization's history, I have a certain pride. To be treated like as inferior, to be forced to work like a field slave until my eyes can no longer see, and to be told it is my own intrinsic fault that I must work so hard—because I am flawed by the sin of being too thorough— becomes more than I can bear.

"Eventually, I knew there would come a time or more when I would have to stand up for myself and risk everything to preserve the brittle nugget of my self-esteem at The Academy…."

*

High noon, September 10, 2009

It's the third day after a naive young physician, straight out of her training, is finally hired. Dr. Leery immediately takes her under his wing and blocks all communication between her and me.

"I hired you because I could control you…."

With the new, young MD on board, I become less indispensable. The chief medical officer, Dr. Furie, appears unannounced at the door of my office when the staff goes off to lunch. Her face is drawn as tense as an executioner. I try to flatter her and comment on her comfortable-looking sweater. She rears in rage, "*What?* Are you saying I don't dress well?"

My finger of friendship tentatively reaches out to touch her shoulder. She recoils in revulsion, jumping back and away from me, squinting her eyelids—the look that I know so well. I am pushed inside a large conference room, filled with some of the cross-cultural art that I'd donated and hung throughout the clinic building to adorn its bleak walls.

Dr. Leery marches in close behind Dr. Furie as if helping to prod a cow. He slams and locks the door behind him. My immediate superior appears nonchalant and dispassionate, carrying a laptop to the conference table and pretending to be absorbed in typing something unrelated to the meeting.

He has an unmistakable smirk on his face.

"I look at my brother in desperation, and he just stands where he is, grinning in frozen silence...."

Dr. Furie tells me to keep quiet and listen to her.

'Don't say anything and don't move!' he orders.

She mechanically begins to rattle a list of mandates:

"Unlike the other physicians, *your* schedule will be completely unblocked and you will see a patient every fifteen minutes without a break and without exception, regardless of the complexity of the care or the acute illnesses of the patient.

"Your caseload is not closed and you will be expected to see even *more* new patients. That will include complex patients—ER and intensive care hospital discharges, or whatever *we decide* to place on your schedule.

"Your working long hours is officially negated as entirely your fault. You are just too thorough. In fact, we do not officially *recognize* your extra hours of work, you have no *proof* of such, and, as far as the medical management is concerned, they did not happen.

"You will only get paid for the contracted twenty-eight hours and you are not officially allowed to work more than that. *Unofficially,* however, you will be expected to continue to work without pay on your days off and on weekends. Remember that physicians have no legal recourse for working sixty or ninety or *more* unpaid hours per week. The administration will graciously and temporarily grant you a private room to do this work during hours of operation on your days off—work that, I remind you, *does not exist.*

"Furthermore, you are not allowed to treat more than one problem per visit."

I interrupt Dr. Furie and describe a typical patient who I'd just seen. He was having signs of a stroke, sudden heart failure with new onset chest pain, untreated Parkinson's Disease with recent loss of ambulation, sudden blindness, newly diagnosed diabetes, terminal renal failure, severe new-onset ipsilateral headaches suggesting an aneurysm, and probable throat cancer.

I ask, "So, which *one* of the deadly problems do I treat on his one visit, the *only* chance to save his life?"

Dr. Furie scoffs mirthfully, "Oh, just give him something for pain and have him come back later for the other problems. *After all, it's the patients' own fault that they're sick!*"

She continues, more vexed because I had dared to speak. "All requests for utilizing your unusual talents are *denied.* The plan for you to case-manage complex medical-psychiatric patients is *revoked.* Emotional problems are irrelevant to the practice of adult medicine. Therefore, you are *not allowed* to treat emotional or psychiatric problems of patients anymore, and you will *not* inquire about their intentions to commit suicide."

A brilliant twenty-seven-year-old University of California graduate had just committed suicide a few weeks before. It would have been prevented if I could have been allowed to spend just a little more time with him. The shock of his death caused ripples of remorse and guilt that I could not overcome. I was discovering an average of two suicidal patients per day, and I had developed a "do no self-harm contract" for them, in several languages, as well as create special protective protocols.

I interrupt her again. "You realize that it is clear malpractice to ignore or not inquire into a patient's emotional state?"

Dr. Furie is losing her grip now. "Furthermore, I hereby order you to *not* order lab tests or studies. If you get abnormal results, you're obligated to do something about them!"

She is making fists and twitching her head. "Our doctors just need to do the bare minimum. We make more money by having patients come back frequently and *not* giving them comprehensive care. Quality is not relevant to the way medicine must be practiced these days! Furthermore, the organization's policy is to provide *access* to care, not *quality* of care. We will continue to advertise that we deliver quality care and we will bill for it. *I order you to stop providing high quality of care!*

"You will be disciplined if you continue to provide quality care. And you will be closely watched. If you make any mistakes because you deviate from optimal quality of care, you will be subjected to still *further* disciplinary action!

"Finally, a gag rule is in place. You are prohibited to talk to any staff member about any matters, about this conversation, or about your working conditions. Talking to the staff upsets them and wastes work time."

I can no longer be myself, be vulnerable, be human, or communicate with the staff on an honest level. The life-threatening, chronic, and disabling problems of patients must be limited to one per visit. The fact that I have no open return slots for six months now means that I must heavily double-book my fifteen-minute slots, or let gravely ill patients just wait until…*I cannot live with a clean conscience.*

At the end of my whipping, Dr. Leery says his only sentence on my behalf, "Nobody in the history of our organization has ever worked anywhere as hard as you have, Dr. King."

Dr. Furie ignores the compliment and glares at him.

The orders begin to echo in my mind. Suddenly, I cannot think, move or function. A record is playing in my head, stuck on the ultimate double bind…

You are *forbidden* to practice quality care medicine, or you will be punished! But if you *don't* practice quality care medicine, you will be punished!

I will be punished no matter what I do!
I will be punished!
I will be punished!
I WILL BE PUNISHED!
I WILL BE PUNISHED!

I CRACK.
I protest vehemently.
I am locked out of the clinic building within three days.
I am told that I am not a good fit for the organization.

I HAVE A NERVOUS BREAKDOWN.
The camel buckles.
Atlas' knees begin to tremble.
The Colossus of Rhodes falls into the sea.

I go on disability and in four months I will start my writing career.

Both poetic prose and expository writing characterize this crucial piece. It is deep and psychologically revealing, without psychologizing—only deep metaphor predominates at the start and end of the segment.

SLAVE RIDDLES:
THE MISFIT MUST FIT IN

Two flanking sphinxes block the portal to freedom through which I will pass. I must solve their lethal riddles:

One sphinx commands me to be unique and ordinary.
The other commands me to fit in and be extraordinary.
BOTH command me to speak my **TRUTH.**

Slave riddles have no apparent solution. As I write, greater and deeper levels of clarity open for me. I am shocked to see the inside of my brain's programming, and at first I don't "see" it, as my mother could not at first "see" her own birth certificate. In retrospect, I wonder why I could not see the obvious…

It was uncanny how I became a slave in nearly every situation I entered, and how psychic bars of inherited oppression blocked my individuation.

A month ago, I realized that the *first* double bind was the obedient field slave ordinance: to perform superhuman work and attain perfection, yet eschew all power. This order had been passed down from field slaves of the intelligentsia, as secret rebels before Emancipation, and later, as moralistic icons and academic geniuses. I had to demonstrate both genius and impeccable obedience to existing social codes of conduct, but be passive, invisible, unrecognized, and humble. Of all these traits, only "humility" is a sane and attainable virtue, in moderation, of course.

The mandate of perfection and powerlessness was designed to subtly prove superiority over whites, yet assure safety by averting white envy and hatred. Perhaps my mother's positive intention was to teach me to be safe in *her* childhood world, in which her narcissistic father's frustrated drive for success and power led to an arrogant demeanor that endangered his family in a racist milieu. I have been told that what whites most fear is an angry black man.

My mother will also remind me of the travails of too much success, the Baptist virtue of humility, and the higher you climb the harder you'll fall—like Icarus. Successful and powerful people get kidnapped for ransom, like the Lindbergh baby, or they get assassinated like Martin Luther King. They even have terrible nightmares.

All my life I have tried to obey the mandate to work hard, march forward and reach for perfection: to "conquer the difficult and almost impossible." I would get within inches from power, recognition, and success, close enough to almost touch it…

And then, I sabotaged my success, pulling myself back into the shadows of failure, over and over. I would forego status, money, and fellowship with the elite to remain in ignominy. My mother learned to suppress and hide her brilliance as she entered young adulthood. Likewise, I was taught to achieve without attracting notice and, therefore, I was subtly banned from *both* power and leadership.

But my mother's advice to hang low was anachronistic in my world; it was a vestige of older times when blacks had to live in the backstage drama of invisibility. I know from my introspection and life experience as a healer that the most devastating effect of shame is a sense of *powerlessness*, which is associated with feeling weak, helpless, and frozen—the definition of a victim.

Now, I vaguely glimpse a *second* double bind that was simultaneously transmitted across many generations, and was implemented centuries before I was born. It pertains to my true core of shame, and it unravels many mysteries about my life process. It was the house slave ordinance: to be unique as an impeccable, mixed race servant that can "fit in" with the white master's family. But, by the nature of slavery, house slaves could not fit in.

Historically, house slaves were marginated as unobtrusive "servant shadows" who had to adapt to and gratify their master's will. They were objects to be exploited in infinitely horrible ways as mere appendages of the master's family—and always inferior to and separate from the elite world of white power.

My mother told me about a chat she had with a wealthy white southerner on a cruise. The lady boasted about how well her ancestors treated their house slaves. "My great-great grandmother even let her favorite house slave woman sleep at the foot of her bed to warm her feet at night!" My mother replied that a dog could do the same.

Nor could house slaves "fit in" with their peers in the field who envied, ostracized and despised them—because they were above field labor and did not suffer constant physical brutality. They had special privileges, like shelter in the big house where they had greater access to, and *sometimes* influence over, the master and his family, even if only by concubinage and miscegenation. They also had material benefits like better food and clothing.

And *ALL* obedient slaves were forbidden the right to have personal boundaries, which are essential for individuation toward a free and unique identity. The obedient field slave was forced to aggregate *en masse* in their shanties and the fields, the predecessor of today's ghettoes, and struggle daily for his or her *physical* survival. The obedient house slave had to become enmeshed with the world of his or her white masters, like most members of today's wage-earning black middle class, and struggle for *psychic* survival.

The only way to establish an independent Self, and the only sane path to follow, was to *rebel*—regardless of the terrible potential consequences one risked. But most slaves were so subjugated by constant vigilance and conditioning from birth that rebellion was not even a thinkable option. Moreover, the attempt to rebel usually failed to reach the goal of manifesting one's true Self, and the ex-slave or slave descendants merely adopted the identity of a slave master by default. The tragic result was that the "rebel" simply acquired narcissistic traits, including ruthless dominance without empathy, self-adulation without altruism, and predatory abuse without compassion.

The patterns of my ancestors designed my domestic life and spread into my social and vocational worlds outside of the home.

My developmental years were in an engulfing and emotionally incestuous home where my parents smothered my independent identity as their house slave. I was the sanctuary for their domestic secrets and their obedient "sleeping angel." I had to manifest special, empathic gifts and deep rapport skills; I had to "read my parent's minds" to survive. These same gifts and skills created a wide-open, boundary-less door to narcissistic predators in my adult life.

I replicated my mother's accursed socialization and become ensnared by her fears. My mother was a misfit in schooling because of her age—a six-year gap from her classmates from age ten to seventeen. I was a misfit because of my race—the first and only non-white in all my schools, from age six to fifteen, and later, due to my lack of early socialization among blacks, I was scorned by my own race as well.

Thereafter, I lived in overlapping worlds of oppression. I was fated to be a house slave pariah, rejected by both envious blacks and domineering whites. I was destined to be a field slave perfectionist, and endure unrewarded toil in abusive jobs. In every milieu, there was a backdrop of psychic or physical danger from volatile environments. The slave traditions led directly to codependency: self-sacrificial *martyrdom* combined with social *margination*. And two of the most devastating long-term effects of slavery are martyrdom and margination.

*

Slave-based riddles are the cornerstone of slavery-acquired behaviors.

The house slave riddle, "You're a misfit, you must fit in" links with the field slave riddle, "Be perfect, avoid success."

Both riddles expand to more and more maddening paradoxes…

"You shall be outstanding, but you must not stand out."

"You are a member of the elite caste, but you must pass as common."

"You must be educated as a genius, but you must never reveal or use your learning and intellect."

And on and on…

I cannot comprehend these double binds, so I must look at them through a refracted lens, or distill them to their essence. I must find the common denominator, the simplified equation of all the slave riddles when they are melted down and fused together.

What I discovered is that they are all based on a false premise: "*The seed of greatness you carry is not normal, and will lead to an endangered and lonely life.*" And that premise leads to a single, absurd solution, which is the essence of all good slaves: **"Be extraordinary, appear ordinary."**

In contradiction to their Baptist virtues, I was taught to commit the cardinal sin: to masquerade, to deceive, or to lie. By feigning ordinariness, I had to play a role and become a hypocrite. To commit this blasphemy demands atonement. And the easiest way to do that is to fail to attain contentment in life.

I will master shame by being relaxed and undefended as I reveal my Truth. I will individuate by remembering that I am connected to Source and have a place in a benevolent cosmos.

Marcel Proust once said: "The most pernicious of all beliefs is that we inhabit a hostile world." That may derive from being cut off from one's cultural legacy and ancestry, one's homeland and familial ties, or one's spirituality and connection to nature, to God, or to the beyond.

Only with both the courage to expose my Truth and my sense of connectedness to a greater whole can I handle the public attention I may receive without danger. I will then stand out as an example of compassion and *not* Narcissism.

This book is a steppingstone toward my life's mission that passes over the stumbling blocks of my shattered identity.

*

VESUVIUS HAS ERUPTED AND POMPEII IS BURIED

I am the volcano and Pompeii's ancient history no longer rules me.
I have reclaimed my anger and resumed my quest for individuation!
My anger is constructive and good; it has neither rancor nor spite.
It had been mysteriously sublimated into fervor in just a few days.

My mother's #1 commandment was to be honest.
Is it honest to *not* reveal one's Truth?
I cannot lie and disguise my Truth.
My Truth must be revealed!

The path to my goal is now clear and irrevocable!
It is barely the dawn of my adventure.

Thor safely lights my way with lightning bolts in a clear sky.
It's time for me to embark.

There is no storm.
The auspices blow toward the Silver City.
I can do repairs *en route* there.
Cut loose the anchor!

The adventure story of my transformative healing is announced.
The bugle horn trumpets.
My fear of death is less than
My fear of life without meaning and purpose.

LET THE DRUMS BEAT RYTHMICALLY HARD AND FAST

This segment extracted from the Epilogue of the original edition ends the book, and is a good summary of the book's social mission. It captures my great-grandfather's book, "I Am a Voice" — in which he recounts both our family history up until the 1920's and the plight of ex-slaves who were dying off by then.

I realized upon writing and researching my genealogy that I've mysteriously, unwittingly, taken over where my ancestors ended— by capturing the ensuing generations and the later effects of slavery.

I AM ALSO A VOICE

My revelations cover the span of lifetimes after my great grandfather, John Wesley Holloway, captured the voices and stories of those who were once slaves and were dying off in the early 1900's. I have attempted to capture the essence of the subsequent generations: those who I knew as a child who are now dead; those who I know who approach death; and those of my generation who are now aging.

Like an anthropologist, I am a voice for several unique populations whose historical existence was largely unknown and whose tenuous presence on Earth might otherwise have been lost. Their experience, as well as my own, may be seen by some as a quirk of the useless past, which is almost as unbelievable as the mutilations, torture and wanton murder of African slaves before Emancipation. Nevertheless, I have given them an immortal voice with valuable lessons for our posterity.

*

I AM A VOICE FOR THE EXCEPTIONAL DESCENDANTS OF SLAVES

From rebellious field slaves rapidly emerged a group that took the freedom of education very seriously. They formed an intelligentsia of genetic brilliance and social defiance, rising to the pinnacles of Academia, law and medicine. Proof of this small cluster of super-achievers starts with my great-great-grandfather's autobiography, a courageous man who learned to read and write in secrecy, risking mortal danger if caught.

I clearly remember my maternal grandfather, who followed his lineage and was among the select few of the field slave descendants to extol and attain academic brilliance—like his own father and grandfather. But his drive for achievement was tainted with a dangerous and self-defensive narcissistic pride, for Reconstruction of the South had failed. Despondent whites would turn their hatred into a merciless backlash, a *whipping* of the entire African-American people for the next century. The "backlash back" was to prove black intellectual superiority over whites, a forerunner of Black Pride.

*

I AM A VOICE FOR THE TRAGIC DESCENDANTS OF SLAVES

The house slaves are also revealed as an eclipsed segment of African-American history, a tiny cluster of humans created by incestuous interbreeding with whites before Emancipation. They were forced to forego all ego and individuality and to fit in with the dominant masters' households, as well as to avert the envious hostility of those who still labored in the fields.

This privileged caste is dying off for many reasons, especially the elimination of color bias and the legality of marriage or sexual liaisons regardless of race or color. Many of them have also died from the probable effects of incest and inter-breeding, lasting hundreds of years as their masters' concubines.

Yet, the worst transgenerational effect upon the descendants of house slaves will span a bit longer. Very few have survived the unspeakable, unimaginable tragedy of behavioral conditioning, for such solipsism is the virtual epitome of pure codependency: To read the master's mind and subjugate one's ego and individuation to him.

My *grandfather* demanded "field slave" perfection of my mother: an absolute and prodigious perfection. It was an edict of enormous pressure to attain the unobtainable, in both scholastic achievement and moral rectitude. My *grandmother* expected my mother to attain a kind of safe status quo as a "house slave": to fit in with unassuming humility. Between the two divergent mandates of her parents, my mother had to simplify the equation to one of disguised perfection: "Be extraordinary, appear ordinary". Thus, she suffered terribly from intrapsychic conflict, chronic depression, and a frustrated, unrewarded genius.

My father is the product of illicit miscegenation, which is another lost lineage of history. Genetic research is revealing in stark disclosure the level of racial intermixing that he represents as an orphan, as a predecessor to the New America—a melting pot of unlimited genetic mixing, which is forever increasing like no other nation on earth.

*

I AM A VOICE FOR MY SELF-HEALING JOURNEY

I am a voice for a rare human experience, witnessing first-hand the beginning of the Civil Rights movement and culminating with an African-American president. I faced the full brunt of racial discrimination, which began as a solitary desegregationist and a mere child in the 1960's. As such, I was the sole recipient of an entire community's focus of envy and hatred.

The combined effects of multiple lines of abuse warped my personal history into one that has few, if any, recorded parallels: the experience of desegregating a northern city's public schools in total isolation of racial peers. I have shown the subtle and pervasive nature of how ancestral slave themes that I learned as a child generalized to house and field slave behavior in new domains, especially in my relationships and my career.

But perhaps I should be indebted to such racial margination, for it provided a unique world perspective as I stood both in the center and on the fringes of many realms, as an observer of the inside action. I came out of the closet in young adulthood, during the beginning of the movement for gay liberation, only to experience prejudice from the "straight people's world" that paralleled that of racism.

Margination also allowed me to be a whistle-blower for the corruption and ethical demise of the medical profession. I debunked the wizard behind the closed curtains of Western medicine, only to find alternative medicine to be just as narcissistic.

I was also a product of elitism. Although I am extremely fortunate to have had an education befitting the ruling class, I could never take advantage of my good fortune. Like a child in a store, or my mother and the dollhouse in the window, I was permitted to look, but not touch. I achieved the fruits of elitist success, but not the permission to eat them.

I hope that my ordeals at home and in my social milieus may be the last generation of Americans to suffer such severe oppression, but I have my doubts. I had to struggle to break the ferocious legacies of both types of slavery to achieve liberation. The omen and the curse, the Slave Riddles and the double binds, a lifetime of abuse and trauma— the spell of *all* had to be broken. It would take over half a century of intense self-work and this book to achieve my ultimate reward: I am finally freed from the transgenerational passage of slavery.

*

I AM A VOICE FOR THE OPPRESSED IN A WORLD OF NEOSLAVERY

Most African-Americans are still enslaved: they are brutally abused as children, and henceforth condemned to inferior status in the massive and enlarging ghettoes of our nation. After training among the ruling class, I could not divest myself of an acquired instinct to be creative and think independently. Because of this, I knew that, eventually, I would break completely free of bondage, and thence, this book-child was born. A grand education was the key to my freedom, but, unfortunately, most African-Americans are unable to benefit from this tool, which slowly, but deeply, digs a path out of the trenches of psychic oppression.

All that I have written is representative of the effects of shame, abuse, trauma and oppression worldwide and which deeply permeate our American culture. The international black struggle against conditions of continued neoslavery is very much like that in America. But the reader must understand that it's not just a matter of black history or African-American history or a personal saga of triumph against shame.

I may be just one of the few that succeeds in the ultimate struggle for identity against historical and developmental chains of conformity to social class structures. Or, I may be another harbinger of a New America or a New World Order—involving a national and international struggle for individual freedom from corporate hegemony.

It is an historical fact that shame-based and abusive conditions haunt almost *every* American, regardless of race, whose roots stem from serfdom, indentured servitude, child-apprentice guilds, prisoner colonies filled with debtors, escapees from refugee camps, and fugitives from fallen, puppet-American governments. And then, there are the billion or more people ardently seeking shelter from cultural or physical annihilation by despots or entrenched ruling classes around the globe.

It is the same neo-slavery that has been imposed on almost all employed workers, the 95% of our population that have been forced out of private enterprise and the professions, to work under the nearly total domination of multi-national corporations.

I have focused on the labor abuse of physicians in this book, since that is my primary knowledge base. The only difference between the displaced and oppressed masses of *other* workers, and that of physicians, is that the latter are held up to the highest ethical standards, the highest academic performance, and suffer the highest levels of stress—now, at the breaking point and *off the edge* of the bell-shaped curve.

*

AM I ALSO A PROPHETIC VOICE OF OUR IMPERILED FUTURE?

It is startling that American childrearing practices and educational systems rely heavily on shame-induction, producing an easily conditioned mass of traumatized adults and passive workers. After reaching the age of the early twenties, almost all Americans succumb to regimented, oppressive structures of social control or become incarcerated in our massive criminal justice system—which I refer to as "placing the mind cap" in this book.

Even more startling and tremendously relevant is the reinstitution of slavery in America.

It is as conspicuous as the widening schism of wealth. It is as subtle as the elimination of the upper middle class, the banishment of the bourgeoisie, and the suppression of the intelligentsia— all of which are now under the cloaked and protected vestments of multinational corporate entities. Social change and revolution cannot be achieved without the leadership of these divested groups.

Many members of these endangered humans are recruited into the prisons of the workforce, or, if defiant, into the ghettoes of our nation. All the warning signs indicating a reversion to a feudal state are present, and now with ever more advanced technologies available to manipulate the human brain.

Fortunately, there are many ways to achieve liberation from oppression and resist the molds of the emerging creators of mass consciousness. Several are alluded to in the metaphors and anecdotes of this book. In this book's sequel, I will share all these methods with the public, for they are powerful and effective. But I offer the reader two clues for now.

First, as we return to our personal, cultural, and spiritual roots, we quickly become much more powerful than an isolated individual who is cut off from the sense of having a place in history. The initial stage of slavery has always been based on the displacement of the slave from his or her ancestral legacy as well as the extended family and village culture that preserves those roots.

Second, a capacity to truly offer romantic love to another, and the blessing of being able to receive unconditional love from another, are the two greatest assets needed in the struggle for the ultimate freedom from shame.

Love is greater than all my techniques.
Love is greater than having the world's best liberal arts education.
Love is greater than any subjugating force in the world.
Love is greater than the combination of all these and more.

*

Carl Jung was a psychic genius. He was also, perhaps, a sage and a prophet. His last word written before Thanatos took him, in his most private and secret "Red Book", is forever:

117

"Possibility"

This book is indeed now done and the finished whole is manifest. All the jigsaw puzzle pieces have been assembled into a *finished* work but not a *complete* work— for I know that the ending of one cycle is accompanied by the birth of a new cycle, and more books are yet to be born.

The struggle, stress and strife of my past have ended. But the future will bring "unknown unknowable's". I have resolved all my major traumas and liberated my soul from its original chains and shackles, but there will be certain, perhaps *greater*, challenges ahead.

The adventure of learning to prevail over shame, abuse, trauma and oppression has no end.

Michael King, MD is a graduate from both Harvard College and Harvard Medical School and he has had over four decades of experience in healthcare and communication skills. His love for biopersonality, consciousness, neuropsychiatry and international health prepared him to explore the essence of human nature.

He specialized in mind-body therapy in his alternative practice, and he has also worked in virtually all aspects of conventional medicine. He is currently a pioneer in social engineering and the first physician to address shame and social oppression, pinpoint their psychobiological roots, and invent treatment programs to resist them.

Dr. King is an expert in writing technology, listening skills, and public speaking, so writing a multi-genre, memoir-driven novel, "Hide and Play Dead," came as naturally as his self-help professional literature in "Overcoming Oppression."

Michael currently has a private practice in psychotherapy and psychiatry in Desert Hot Springs, California where he specializes in the treatment of shame, abuse, trauma, and social oppression. His treatment process is based on high empathy, high rapport, client-centered approaches, along with somatic therapy and non-invasive emerging technologies in the neurosciences.

His current writing project is a study manual and workbook to accompany "Overcoming Oppression." A guide to his treatment system for healthcare professionals will soon follow—representing a paradigm shift for most of the social sciences and the field of medicine.

"It is time for the healer to emerge from the walls of clinical medicine and tackle the social milieu where illness is perpetuated. It is time for a new and revolutionary branch of medicine to take a stand against the primary source of human suffering in the world today."

9 781981 244027